W0393718

New Edition

Viewfinder

Topics

Gender Roles

Equal but Different?

compiled and edited by
Annegret Schrick

Langenscheidt

Berlin · München · Wien · Zürich · New York

Viewfinder

Topics

Unterrichtsmaterialien für die Sekundarstufe II

Gender Roles

Equal but Different?

Herausgeber:
Prof. em. Dr. Dr. h.c. Dr. h.c. Peter Freese, Paderborn

Autorin:
Dr. Annegret Schrick

Projekt-Team:
Dr. Martin Arndt, Münster
David Beal, M. A., Bochum
Cornelia Becker, Bremen
Dr. Peter Dines, Cert. Ed., Ludwigsburg
Prof. i. R. Dr. Hanspeter Dörfel, Ludwigsburg
OStR Dieter Düwel, Castrop-Rauxel
Prof. em. Dr. Dr. h.c. Dr. h.c. Peter Freese, Paderborn
Dr. Carin Freywald †
Jennifer von der Grün, B. A., Dortmund
OStR Ulrich Imig, Wildeshausen
OStR Reimer Jansen, Oyten-Sagehorn
Dr. Michael Mitchell, M. A., Reken und Warwick
Prof. Dr. Michael Porsche, Paderborn
StD i. E. Detlef Rediker, Lippstadt
StD Dr. Peter-J. Rekowski, Kirchhain
OStR i.K. Peter Ringeisen, M. A., Amberg
Karl Sassenberg, Münster
StD Henning Scholz †
StD Dr. Annegret Schrick, Essen
OStR Ekkehard Sprenger, Kiel
OStD Dr. Dietrich Theißen, Gütersloh
Donald Turner, M. A. †
Prof. Dr. Laurenz Volkmann, Jena
Philip Wade, M. A., Cert. Ed., Amberg

Verlagsredaktion: Dr. Beatrix Finke
Visuelles Konzept, Layout und Produktion: Barbara Slowik, Atelier S., München

www.langenscheidt.de/viewfinder

Umwelthinweis: Gedruckt auf chlorfrei gebleichtem Papier.

1. Auflage 2007

© 2007 Langenscheidt KG, Berlin und München

Das Werk und seine Teile sind urheberrechtlich geschützt. Jede Verwertung in anderen als den gesetzlich zugelassenen Fällen bedarf deshalb der vorherigen schriftlichen Einwilligung des Verlages.

Druck: Druckhaus Berlin-Mitte GmbH, Berlin
Printed in Germany

ISBN 978-3-526-50732-1

1 2 3 4 5 / 11 10 09 08 07

Contents

* Titles provided by the editor

Gender Roles

When we look at the world around us we see men and women, boys and girls, male and female, her and him, we see identity and otherness. It has been widely agreed in gender studies that gender is the social construction of male/female identity. Most people experience gender as "an emergent feature of social situations: as both an outcome of and a rationale for various social arrangements" (West/Zimmermann, 1991).[1)] It can be seen as a set of ideas which influence male/female behaviour, a set of signs and symbols and a principle governing social organisation.

The term 'gender' itself is not very old. It came into existence in the course of the second-wave feminism beginning in the 1960s, in the wake of the Civil Rights Movement and world-wide protest marches. The theoretical concept was based on three principles. On the one hand the construct of gender is seen as flexible in contrast to the biological category of sex which is fixed. Secondly, both concepts presuppose the binary oppositions of male/female. And finally, there is a strong interaction between gender and other relevant categories such as race and class so much so that gender becomes the central criterion through which power structures can be explained.[2)] But how is gender-specific behaviour projected on to the social being? The question has reopened the discussion about nature vs. nurture. Are behavioural differences the result of learning and conditioning or of emulation and imitation? How much of gender-specific behaviour can be attributed to people's genetic make-up and how much to their socialisation? Although on the surface level the characteristics associated with *male-ness* and *female-ness* give the impression of being 'natural' or biologically founded, they are – in fact – socially constructed and variable. Due to the fact that gender can only be understood in a social context the increasingly rapid change within this social context will have a decisive influence on the flexibility of gender roles in our modern world. To understand its essence we must first look at developments having

[1)] West, Candace & Don H. Zimmermann (1991), "Doing Gender", in Susan Lorber & Judith Farell, eds., *The Social Construction of Gender,* Newbury Park - London - New Delhi: Sage Publiucations, 13-34. – [2)] cf. von Rosenberg, Ingrid (2006), "Gender in der britischen Gesellschaft" in Hans Kastendiek et al., eds., *Länderbericht Großbritannien,* Berlin: Bundeszentrale für politische Bildung.

Equal but Different?

What are little boys made of?
What are little boys made of?
Frogs and snails
And puppy dog's tails.
That's what little boys are made of.
What are little girls made of?
What are little girls made of?
Sugar and spice
And all that's nice
That's what little girls are made of.
(Anonymous)

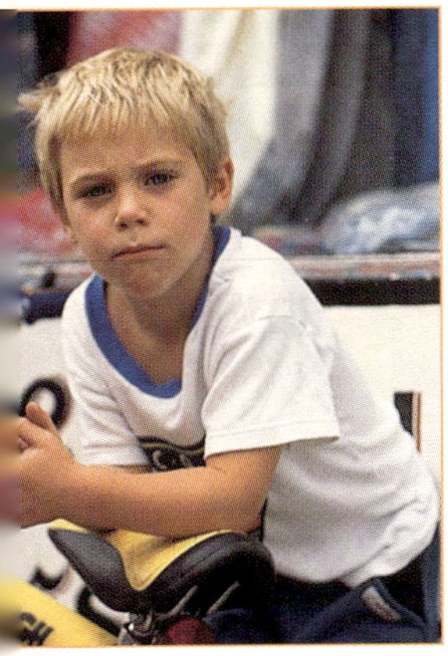

evolved over long periods of time. How can **the** male gender role be defined? Is it that of the cowboy roaming through the Wild West, of the New Superdad or rather of metros like Robbie Williams and friends, cultivating their female side? What is the definition of **the** female gender role? Is it that of the suffragette on hunger strike, of the devoted mommy or of the "female chauvinist pig" of the 21st century? Or could it be that it is a little bit of everything and that not only have we become more tolerant, but also more flexible in our concept of gender roles, so flexible even that we can allow scope for playfulness and experiment? Could it be that the semiotics of behaviour, clothes and outward appearance are by no means as clear as they used to be, thus making their interpretation more complex, but more rewarding at the same time? Perhaps it will eventually help woman to get in touch with her 'inner man', and man with his 'inner woman'.

Child's letter from Children's Letters to God

1

Mark Twain

"Boy or Girl?"*

The following is an excerpt from Mark Twain's novel *The Adventures of Huckleberry Finn* (1884). Huck, the young hero, has very adult problems: together with an escaped slave, Jim, he is floating down the Mississippi on a raft. During their trip, Huck learns about the evils of the world. This departure from innocence is seen as an integral part of the process of growing up. – Mark Twain, *The Adventures of Huckleberry Finn* (London: Harrap & Co, 1924), pp. 73ff.

The woman kept looking at me pretty curious, and I didn't feel a bit comfortable. Pretty soon she says: "What did you say your name was, honey?"

"M – – Mary Williams."

Somehow it didn't seem to me that I said it was Mary before, so I didn't look up; seemed to me I said it was Sarah; so I felt sort of cornered, and was afeared maybe I was looking it, too. I wished the woman would say something more; the longer she set still, the uneasier I was. But now she says: "Honey, I thought you said it was Sarah, when you first come in?"

"Oh, yes'm, I did. Sarah Mary Williams. Sarah's my first name. Some calls me Sarah, some calls me Mary."

"Oh, that's the way of it?"

"Yes'm."

I was feeling better then, but I wished I was out of there, anyway. I couldn't look up yet.

Well, the woman fell to talking about how hard times was, and how poor they had to live, and how the rats was as free as if they owned the place, and so forth, and so on, and then I got easy again. She was right about the rats. You'd see one stick his nose out of a hole in the corner every little while. She said she had to have things handy to throw at them when she was alone, or they wouldn't give her no peace. She showed me a bar of lead, twisted up into a knot, and said she was a good shot with it generly, but she'd wrenched her arm a day or two ago, and didn't know, whether she could throw true, now. But she watched for a chance, and directly she banged away at a rat, but she missed him wide, and said "Ouch!" it hurt her arm so. Then she told me to try for the next one. I wanted to be getting away before the old man got back but of course I didn't let on. I got the thing and the first rat that showed his nose I let drive, and if he'd a stayed where he was he'd been a tolerable sick rat. She said that that was first rate, and she reckoned I would hive the next one. She went and got the lump of lead and fetched it back and brought along a hank of yarn, which she wanted me to help her with. I held up my two hands and she put the hank over then [sic] and went on talking about her and her husband's matters. But she broke off to say: "Keep your eye on the rats. You better have the lead in your lap, handy."

So she dropped the lump into my lap, just at that moment, and I clapped my legs together on it and she went on talking. But only about a minute. Then she took off the hank and looked me straight in the face, but very pleasant and says: "Come, now – What's your real name?"

"Wh–what, mum?"

"What's your real name? Is it Bill, or Tom, or Bob? – or what is it ?"

I reckon I shook like a leaf, and I didn't know hardly what to do. But I says: "Please to don't poke fun at a poor girl like me, mum. If I'm in the way here, I'll – –"

"No, you won't. Set down and stay where you are. I ain't going to hurt you, and I ain't going to tell on you, nuther. You just tell me your secret, and trust me. I'll keep it; and what's more, I'll help you. So'll my old man, if you want him to. You see, you're a runaway 'prentice – that's all. It ain't anything. There ain't any harm in it. You've been treated bad, and you made up your mind to cut. Bless you, child, I wouldn't tell on you. Tell me all about it, now – that's a good boy."

So I said it wouldn't be no use to try to play it any longer, and I would just make a clean breast and tell everything, but she mustn't go back on her promise. Then I told her my father and mother was dead, and the law had bound me out to a mean old farmer in the country thirty mile back from the river, and he treated me so bad I couldn't stand it no longer; he went away to be gone a couple of days, and so I took my chance and stole some of his daughter's old clothes, and cleared out, and I had been three nights coming the thirty miles; I travelled nights, and hid day-times and slept, and the bag of bread and meat I carried from home lasted me all the way and I had a plenty. I said I believed my uncle Abner Moore would take care of me.

Info

Language note

In his novel Mark Twain imitates Mid-Western and Southern dialects. He explains this in a note to the reader, claiming that the shadings of these dialects have been elaborated "with the trustworthy guidance and support of personal familiarity with these several forms of speech." It is still true today that Southerners are readily identified by their speech. Yet the South is more diverse in speech than any other region of the country, with the most distinctive varieties found in isolated areas.

13 some calls me: Mid-Western dialect for some call me - **25 they wouldn't give her no peace**: they wouldn't give her any peace - **27 generly** (adv.): generally - **39f. he'd a stayed**: he would have stayed - **64 I ain't going to**: I am not going to - **65 nuther**: neither

Vocabulary

3 honey (n.): (AmE) used informally as a friendly form of address, esp. by or to a woman - **7 to corner** (v.): to force (a person or animal) into a difficult or threatening position - **7 afeared** (adj.): (archaic) afraid - **12 yes'm**: colloquial for "yes, madam" - **18 to fall to doing s.th.** (v.): here: to begin - **26 lead** (n.): /led/ a soft, heavy, easily melted, greyish-blue metal, used for waterpipes, to cover roofs, etc. - **26f. a good shot**: a person who aims with great skill - **27 to wrench** (v.): to twist and damage (a joint of the body) - **28 to throw true**: to throw exactly, not missing the target - **33 to let on** (v.): informal for to tell a secret - **37 to hive** (v.): to lay up in store - **38 hank** (n.): a coil of a specified length, varying with the type of yarn - **39 yarn** (n.): (esp. AmE) a long continuous usually cotton or woollen thick thread used in knitting, etc. - **49 mum**: here: madam; a term of reverence used by a younger to an older person - **59 'prentice** (n.): short for apprentice, a person who is under an agreement to work for a person who is skilled in a trade, in order to learn that person's skill - **63 that's a good boy**: used when telling or persuading a child to do s.th. - **65 to make a clean breast of**: to tell the whole truth about (s.th. bad that one has done)

Explanations

67 the law had bound me out: A male orphan, being a ward of the state, could by law be bound as an apprentice from the age of fourteen until he reached twenty-one years of age. - **69 the river**: the Mississippi

Info

Gender socialization

If human behaviour and the attitudes and practices associated with male and female roles are not innate or biologically produced, but are the consequence of culture, then, it is argued, they have to be learned. The process by which any new recruits into any given society learn their gender roles is called socialization (see also p. 9).

Sociology, ed. by Jane L. Thompson, Judith Priestley (London: Butterworth-Heinemann, 1996)

Samuel Langhorne Clemens ('Mark Twain') (1835-1910), born in Hannibal, Missouri, followed the printer's trade in Eastern and Middle-Western cities; journeyed down to New Orleans intending to make his fortune in Brazil, but abandoned the scheme and became a Mississippi river-pilot instead. After a short period as a Confederate volunteer, he spent the remainder of the Civil War years in Nevada and San Francisco, writing humorous newspaper items under the pseudonym of 'Mark Twain'. In 1870, he married Olivia Langdon, and soon settled with her in Hartford, Connecticut. He wrote many books, nearly all well-received, including *The Adventures of Tom Sawyer* (1876), *Life on the Mississippi* (1883), and *The Adventures of Huckleberry Finn* (1884). When Mark Twain had completed his first boy's story, *The Adventures of Tom Sawyer*, he wrote: "By and by I shall take a boy of twelve and run him through life (in the first person), but not Tom Sawyer; he would not make a good character for it." This is how *The Adventures of Huckleberry Finn* was born. In the novel, Huck is facing a serious moral problem: the laws of society say he must return the escaped slave Jim to his owner. But Huck decides that the slave is a man, not a "thing"; Huck thinks deeply about morality and then decides to break the law. After that he is not a child any more.

Awareness

1 When you were a boy/girl what toys did you play with? Were your toys considered appropriate for your sex?

2 Try the following experiment: Throw a tennis ball into the laps of one of your female and one of your male fellow students and closely observe their reaction. Take notes of your observations and compare them in class.

Comprehension

3 What is the confusion about the girl's names?

4 What is meant by "I felt cornered?" (l. 7)

5 Why do Huck and the old lady aim at some rats?

6 What is the reason the old lady puts forth for not being able to aim properly?

7 How does the old lady know that Huck is not a girl?

8 Why does the old lady want to help him?

9 Why does Huck pretend to be a girl?

Analysis

10 Characterize the relationship between Huck and the old lady.

11 The entire episode is based on alternating feelings of trust and distrust. Analyse how they are indicated in the text.

12 What effect does the first-person singular point of view have?

Opinion

13 Would you have known that Huck is not a girl?

14 If you were the old lady, would you hand Huck over to the authorities? Give reasons for your opinion.

15 Imagine that the old lady's husband returns. Try to make up what she tells him.

Project

16 Making use of the background information on pp. 7 and 9 give a written evaluation of the factors that influence gender stereotyping and on the chances of overcoming it.

Suggested Further Reading

17 If you want to find out about the behaviour of boys nowadays, read Roddy Doyle's *Paddy Clarke, Ha Ha Ha* (London: Minerva, 1993), which will also give you an idea of gender differences in reading and thus may serve as a link with the facts presented in the next text.

Info

'Gender'

refers to ways of seeing and representing people and situations based on sex difference. By contrast, 'sex' is a biological category: female or male. The term 'sexuality' refers to the realm of sexual experience and desire - sometimes it refers to a person's sexual orientation (as heterosexual, bisexual or homosexual). 'Gender' is a social or cultural category, influenced by stereotypes about 'male' and 'female' behaviour that exist in our attitudes and beliefs. Such beliefs are often said to be 'culturally produced' or 'constructed'.

[...] We are all aware of some degree of cultural stereotyping about gender. For instance many of us will be familiar with the Western tradition of designating colours to signify sex difference; 'pink for girls, blue for boys'. In providing visual symbols for sex difference, we allow for imaginative and interpretative associations attached to those colours: pink perhaps suggesting softness and 'girlishness' and blue suggesting 'boyishness'. While the designations 'female' and 'male' are sex categories, the imaginative ideas associated with these differences include a range of cultural and individualized ideas about gender. Preconceptions about gender might include the idea that 'women drivers' are in some way less able than 'drivers' (assumed to be male), or the notion that 'big boys don't cry'. Further examples might include giving boys bigger portions of food or giving boys trucks rather than dolls as gifts. In the world of work, there is the gendered division of labour, characterized by a striking male domination of high status, highly paid areas of work. So, gender can be read in sexual stereotypes and in power relations between individuals and groups. In the process of studying these phenomena, we engage with symbolic ideas attached to sex difference (colours, ideas, images) which involve our imaginations and interpretative skills. If we read with concern for identifying assumptions and stereotypes about gender, we learn about society as well as about literature.

Literature and Gender, *ed. by Lizbeth Goodman (London: Routledge, 1996), pp. vii f.*

2 Gender and the three R's: The development of literacy achievement by girls and boys *

A lot of controversy has developed over the issue of education, when it became obvious that girls were ahead of boys in many areas of the school curriculum and that boys seemed to have an aversion against reading. Among other aspects this aversion seems to have been counteracted by the attraction that TV and computer games exert on boys. - *Language and Society*, ed. by George Keith and John Shuttleworth (Hodder & Stoughton: London, 2004).

Educational theorists are beginning to think that girls and boys learn differently, and to assure that all achieve equally, new teaching and learning strategies need to be developed. [...]

Statistics suggest that by the age of six girls are reading more than boys and that the trend continues for life. Despite of the fact that 90% of homes have books, and that almost all parents say that they read to their children, as girls mature into adults they continue to read substantially more than men.

What do girls and boys read? Boys enjoy comics and graphic novels, girls like fiction and poetry, and between 15 and 16 girls prefer magazines to books. The lowest level for reading amongst young men and women is in the 18-19 age group. Women's reading recovers from this dip, men's doesn't. Girls are three times more likely to use the public library than boys, and women between 25 and 34 read, borrow or buy four times more books than men. Women are sociable readers and enjoy discussion groups, something relatively rare among men.

The most recent concern for educators is boys' poor performance in the literacy skills (reading, writing, speaking, listening), although the 1997 Labour government's 'Literacy Hour' is helping to combat this. At primary level in 1998 boys were much less successful than girls in the junior reading test: their performance improved by 14% in 1999, although this may have been because it seemed a more 'boy-friendly' examination, with clear-cut questions and factual answers (it was about spiders!).

There were concerns about girls' secondary school performance in the 1970s and 1980s. [...] There are more concerns for educators looking beyond secondary education to m/f employment, though Curriculum 2000 is intended to help, with its emphasis on key skills. Girls still have lower career aspirations, and 61% of all working women are employed in low status, low-earning jobs, following traditional gendered job stereotypes.

A good read: one of life's simple pleasures

Vocabulary

9 to mature (v.): to become fully grown or developed - **12 graphic novel** (n.): a novel whose narrative is related through a combination of text and art, often in comic-strip form - **16 dip** (n.): a slight decrease in the amount of s.th. - **19 sociable** (adj.): friendly, enjoying other people's company - **22 literacy** (n.): the state of being able to read and write - **24 to combat** (v.): to try to stop s.th. bad from happening or getting worse - **36 aspiration** (n., usually pl.): a strong desire to have or achieve s.th.

Explanations

Title: **three R's**: reading, writing and arithmetic, considered as forming the base of children's education - **24 Literacy Hour**: a scheme introduced by the British government to raise standards of literacy - **35 key skills**: The Department for Education and Skills (DfES) defines key skills as a range of essential skills that underpin success in education, employment, lifelong learning and personal development.

Awareness

1 Do you regularly use your school or the public library? Why (not)?
2 What reading materials do you use? Make a list of all the texts you have read in the course of a week. Which have you read for pleasure? Compare your list with others.
3 Do you think it is important to read bedtime stories to a child? Give reasons.

Comprehension

4 What do the statistics reveal about different reading habits among boys and girls?
5 How do their reading habits change in later life?
6 To what extent may reading habits influence career prospects?

Project

7 Design a curriculum for a school of your choice. Which subjects, if any, would you teach to girls, which to boys, which co-educationally?

Internet Projects

8 Go to www.aas.duke.edu/admin/curriculum2000/report.html and find out about the areas covered in the National Curriculum and what methods the government has developed to raise the level of literacy.
9 Find out about key skills and check whether there are similar concepts in German education. http://www.dfes.gov.uk/keyskills/what.shtml might help you.

3 "The Seneca Falls Convention"

The Seneca Falls Convention in 1848 marked the beginning of an organized women's movement in the U.S.A. Most of its members came from middle-class native-born families in small towns in the North and Midwest with strong reform movements. With the Declaration of Independence as their rhetorical model and ideological justification, the Declaration of Sentiments was approved by the convention and signed by 68 women and 32 men. – *The Feminist Papers: From Adams to de Beauvoir*, ed. by Alice Rossi (New York: Bantam, 1974), pp. 415-418.

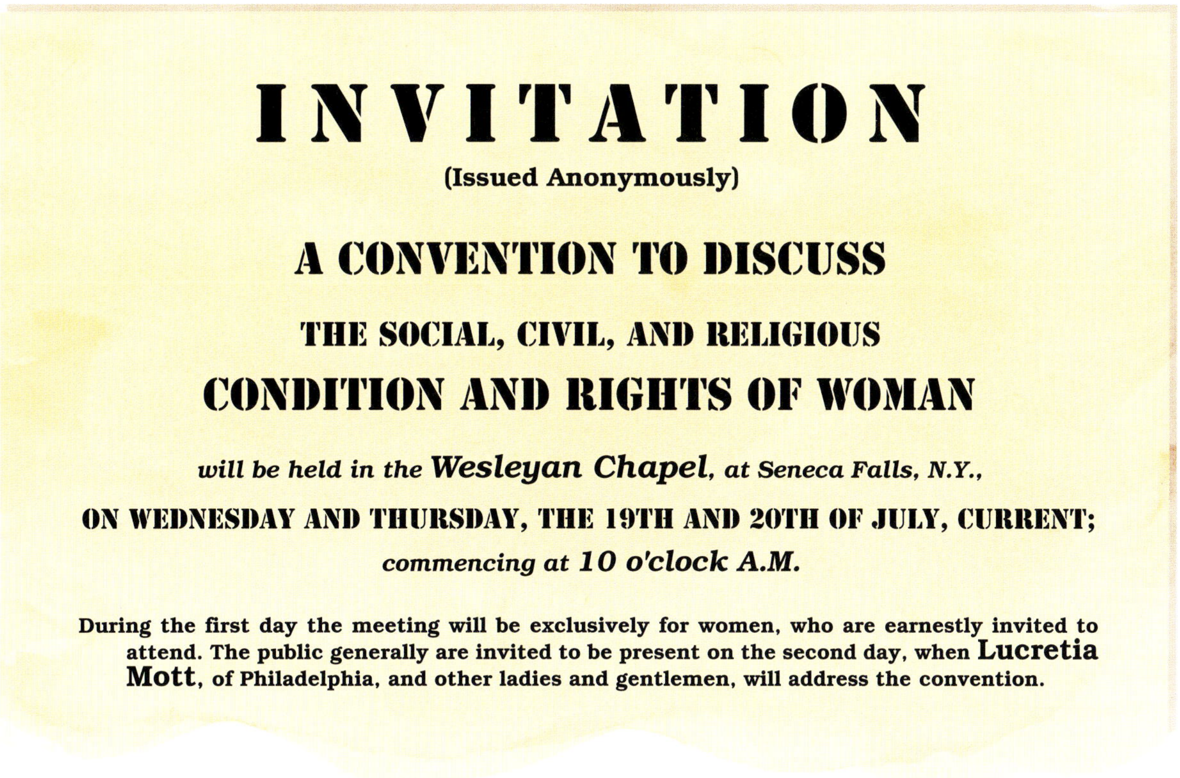

INVITATION

(Issued Anonymously)

A CONVENTION TO DISCUSS

THE SOCIAL, CIVIL, AND RELIGIOUS

CONDITION AND RIGHTS OF WOMAN

***will be held in the* Wesleyan Chapel, *at* Seneca Falls, N.Y.,**

ON WEDNESDAY AND THURSDAY, THE 19TH AND 20TH OF JULY, CURRENT;

***commencing at* 10 o'clock A.M.**

During the first day the meeting will be exclusively for women, who are earnestly invited to attend. The public generally are invited to be present on the second day, when Lucretia Mott, of Philadelphia, and other ladies and gentlemen, will address the convention.

The Feminist Papers: From Adams to de Beauvoir, ed. by Alice Rossi (New York: Bantam, 1974), p. 413

When, in the course of human events, it becomes necessary for one portion of the family of man to assume among the people of the earth a position different from that which they have hitherto occupied, but one to which the laws of nature and of nature's God entitle them, a decent respect to the opinions of mankind requires that they should declare the causes that impel them to such a course.

We hold these truths to be self-evident: that all men and women are created equal; that they are endowed by their Creator with certain inalienable rights; that among these are life, liberty, and the pursuit of happiness; that to secure these rights governments are instituted, deriving their just powers from the consent of the governed. Whenever any form of government becomes destructive of these ends, it is the right of those who suffer from it to refuse allegiance to it, and to insist upon the institution of a new government, laying its foundation on such principles, and organizing its powers in such form, as to them shall seem most likely to effect their safety and happiness. [...]

The history of mankind is a history of repeated injuries and usurpations on the part of man toward woman, having in direct object the establishment of an absolute tyranny over her. To prove this, let facts be submitted to a candid world.

He has never permitted her to exercise her inalienable right to the elective franchise.

He has compelled her to submit to laws, in the formation of which she had no voice.

He has withheld from her the rights which are given to the most ignorant and degraded men – both natives and foreigners.

Having deprived her of this first right of a citizen, the elective franchise, thereby leaving her without representation in the halls of legislation, he has oppressed her on all sides.

He has made her, if married, in the eye of the law, civilly dead.

The second class status of women (as well as other groups) is dramatized in this poster titled American Woman and Her Political Peers, *showing Frances Willard surrounded by a mentally handicapped man, a convict, a Native American, and an insane man.*

He has taken from her all right in property, even to the wages she earns.

He has made her, morally, an irresponsible being, as she can commit many crimes with impunity, provided they be done in the presence of her husband. In the covenant of marriage, she is compelled to promise obedience to her husband, he becoming, to all intents and purposes, her master – the law giving him power to deprive her of her liberty, and to administer chastisement.

He has so framed the laws of divorce, as to what shall be the proper causes, and in case of separation, to whom the guardianship of the children shall be given, as to be wholly regardless of the happiness of women – the law, in all cases, going upon a false supposition of the supremacy of man, and giving all power into his hands.

After depriving her of all rights as a married woman, if single, and the owner of property, he has taxed her to support a government which recognizes her only when her property can be made profitable to it.

He has monopolized nearly all the profitable employments, and from those she is permitted to follow, she receives but a scanty remuneration. He closes against her all the avenues to wealth and distinction which he considers most honorable to himself. As a teacher of theology, medicine, or law, she is not known.

He has denied her the facilities for obtaining a thorough education, all colleges being closed against her.

He allows her in Church, as well as State, but a subordinate position, claiming Apostolic authority for her exclusion from the ministry, and, with some exceptions, from any public participation in the affairs of the Church.

He has created a false public sentiment by giving to the world a different code of morals for men and women, by which moral delinquencies which exclude women from society, are not only tolerated, but deemed of little account in man.

He has usurped the prerogative of Jehovah himself, claiming it as his right to assign for her a sphere of action, when that belongs to her conscience and to her God.

He has endeavored, in every way that he could, to destroy her confidence in her own powers, to lessen her self-respect, and to make her willing to lead a dependent and abject life.

Now, in view of this entire disfranchisement of one-half the people of this country, their social and religious degradation – in view of the unjust laws above mentioned, and because women do feel themselves aggrieved, oppressed, and fraudulently deprived of their most sacred rights, we insist that they have immediate admission to all the rights and privileges which belong to them as citizens of the United States.

[There follow a number of resolutions of which the following three may serve as examples:]

Resolved, That such laws as conflict, in any way, with the true and substantial happiness of woman, are contrary to the great precept of nature and of no validity, for this is "superior in obligation to any other."

Resolved, That all laws which prevent woman from occupying such a station in society as her conscience shall dictate, or which place her in a position inferior to that of man, are contrary to the great precept of nature, and therefore of no force or authority.

Resolved, That woman is man's equal – was intended to be so by the Creator, and the highest good of the race demands that she should be recognized as such.

Designed by the suffragettes in Britain, this peaceful propaganda poster alerts the public to the government's irrational stand against women.

Vocabulary

2 to assume (v.): to take or claim for o.s. - **4 hitherto** (adv.): formal for: up until now - **6 decent** (adj.): proper, socially acceptable - **7 to impel** (v.): to force - **10 to be endowed with** (v.): to possess from time of birth - **11 inalienable rights** (n.): rights which cannot be taken away - **12 pursuit** (n.): /pəˈsjuːt/ aim, effort towards s.th. - **13 to secure** (v.): to make certain that one gets s.th. - **17 allegiance** (n.): loyalty, faith, and dutiful support to a leader, country, idea, etc. - **23 usurpation** (n.): formal for the act of taking (power or position) for o.s. illegally or without having the right to do so - **24 object** (n.): purpose; aim - **25f. to submit** (v.): to offer for consideration - **26 candid** (adj.): open, honest, and sincere in manner - **28 franchise** (n.): the right to vote in a public election, esp. one held to choose a parliament - **31 to withhold from** (v.): to keep back on purpose; to refuse to give - **32 degraded** (adj.): without self-respect or the good opinion of other people - **36 halls of legislation**: corridors of power, where laws are made - **39 civilly** (adv.): in accordance with civil law - **46f. with impunity** (n.): without any danger of being punished - **50 covenant** (n.): a formal solemn agreement between two or more people or groups - **53f. to all intents and purposes**: in almost every way; very nearly - **58 to administer** (v.): formal for to give; dispense - **58 chastisement** (n.): /tʃæˈstaɪzmənt/ punishment, esp. by beating - **63 separation** (n.): (law) a formal agreement by a husband and wife to live apart - **64 guardianship** (n.): the position of being responsible for someone else's child - **70 supremacy** (n.): the state of being supreme; having the highest position, in terms of power, importance, or influence - **79 but** (adv.): esp. literary for only - **79 scanty** (adj.): hardly enough in size or quantity - **79 remuneration** (n.): formal for payment - **80 avenue** (n.): a means of reaching a desired result - **86 subordinate** (adj.): of a lower rank or position - **86 apostolic** (adj.): of or concerning one of Christ's 12 apostles - **87 ministry** (n.): priests, considered as a group or profession - **91 delinquency** (n.): behaviour that is not in accordance with accepted social standards or the law - **92 to deem** (v.): formal for to consider - **93 account** (n.): importance - **94 to usurp** (v.): formal for to take (power or position) for o.s. illegally or without having the right to do so - **94 prerogative** (n.): a special right belonging to a particular person - **94 Jehovah** (n.): a name given to God in the Old Testament - **96 to assign** (v.): to give as a share or duty - **100 to endeavor** (v.): formal for to try - **107 object** (adj.): formal for (of a condition) as low as possible; pitiful - **109 disfranchisement** (n.): state of having been deprived of the franchise - **116f. aggrieved** (adj.): showing hurt, angry, and bitter feelings, esp. because one has been unfairly treated - **118 fraudulently** (adv.): deceitfully; got or done by fraud

Explanations

5 the laws of nature and of nature's God: *The Declaration* reflects the work of 17th and 18th century philosophers, particularly of John Locke (1632-1704). In 1690 he published *Two Treatises of Government*. In the first he refuted the divine right of kings and justified revolution. In the second he maintained that men have natural rights which government cannot interfere with or deprive them of because they are based on the unchangeable laws of nature or of God.

The first modern woman's rights convention, called through the initiative of **Lucretia Coffin Mott** (1793-1880) and Elizabeth Cady Stanton (1815-1902), was held in the Wesleyan Chapel at Seneca Falls, N.Y., on 19 and 20 July 1848 (see the *Invitation* on p. 11). At the gathering a declaration of sentiments (modelled after the American Declaration of Independence) listing the many discriminations existing against women was read, and a series of eleven resolutions, one of them calling for woman suffrage, were adopted. Stanton was the leader of the American Women's Movement. Together with Susan B. Anthony (1820-1906) she demanded better education for women, a reformation of marriage laws, and legal equality. Between 1865 and 1893 she was president of the National Woman Suffrage Association; in 1888 she presided over the first International Women's Conference in Washington. The social reformers Mott, Stanton, and Anthony together were also called the invincible giants of early feminism. All three were agreed on the fact that that "the question of marriage was the foundation of all reforms for women".

Awareness

1 What motivated the American "Founding Fathers" to sign *The Declaration of Independence* in 1776?
2 Compare the two illustrations (pp. 12 and 13) and state common traits of the suffrage movements in Britain and the U.S.

Comprehension

3 What is meant by "one portion of the family of man" (l. 2) in the context of *The Declaration of Sentiments*?
4 What is the function of governments, according to the authors of *The Declaration of Sentiments*?
5 What is the right of those who are subject to a government?
6 How do the authors of *The Declaration of Sentiments* view the relation between men and women?
7 Re-write the 15 complaints starting with "He ..." (l. 27) in the form of demands.

Analysis

8 Analyse the use of language in the *Declaration* and classify the register.
9 Compare *The Declaration of Sentiments* to *The Declaration of Independence:* what are the similarities of the concerns reflected in the documents ?
10 One of the best-known, possibly the best-known, quotations from *The Declaration of Independence* is that "all men are created equal". Compare the associations the Founding Fathers had with the word "men" with the associations of the early feminists and define the difference. Make use of the background information, given on p. 15.

Opinion

11 Do you think it was a good idea to model *The Declaration of Sentiments* upon *The Declaration of Independence*? Give reasons for your opinion.
12 One spin-off of the Seneca Falls Convention was the women's suffrage movement. However, class and race differences made it difficult for women to unite. Working in groups, decide whether you would have joined the women's suffrage movement if you had been a black woman in the South or a female factory worker in the North.

Project

13 Design a pamphlet to be circulated by the press in which you propagate the most important of your demands (see exercise 7).

Internet Project

14 We have currently reached a phenomenon called Third Wave Feminism. Find out about its principles and policies. The following site might help you: http://womensissues.about.com/cs/feminism/f/thirdwave_p.htm.

Background Information

The early American Woman's Rights Movement (W.R.M.) was radical. In the 19th century for women to attack the Family, the Church (see Elizabeth Cady Stanton's *Woman's Bible*), and the State (law) was for them to attack the very cornerstones of the Victorian society in which they lived - equivalent to attacking sex distinctions themselves in our time. The theoretical foundations of the early W.R.M. grew out of the most radical ideas of the day. Few people today are aware of the fact that early feminism was a true grass-roots movement. They have not heard of the torturous journeys made by feminist pioneers into backwoods and frontiers, or door to door in the towns to speak about the issues or to collect signatures for petitions that were laughed right out of the Assemblies. Nor do they know that Elizabeth Cady Stanton and Susan B. Anthony, the most militant feminists of the movement, were among the first to stress the importance of organizing women workers, founding the Working Woman's Association in September, 1868. [...]

This radical movement was built by women who had literally no civil status under the law; who were pronounced civilly dead upon marriage, or who remained legal minors if they did not marry; who could not sign a will or even have custody of their own children upon divorce; who were not taught even to read, let alone admitted to college (the most privileged of them were equipped with a knowledge of embroidery, china painting, French, and harpsichord); who had no political voice whatever. Thus, even after the Civil War, more than half this country's population was legally enslaved, literally not owning even the bustles on their backs.

The first stirrings of this oppressed class, the first simple demands for justice, were met by a disproportionate violence, a resistance difficult to understand today when the lines of sexual class have been blurred over. For, as often happens, the revolutionary potential of the first awakening was recognized more clearly by those in power than it was by the crusaders themselves. From its very beginning the feminist movement posed a serious threat to the established order, its very existence and long duration testifying to fundamental inequalities in a system that pretended to democracy. Working first together, later separately, the Abolitionist Movement and the W.R.M. threatened to tear the country apart.

Shulamith Firestone, "On American Feminism," *Woman in Sexist Society: Studies in Power and Powerlessness*, ed. by Vivian Gornick & Barbara K. Moran (New York: Mentor, 1972), pp. 666f.

Did You Know?

U.S.A., 1920

Women allowed to vote - for the first time in history!

G.B., 1970

British law requires: Equal pay for women.

G.B., 1927

No more hunger strikes! Women allowed to the ballot!

G.B., 1975

Wives allowed to open bank accounts without husband's consent

U.S.A., 1964

Another victory for womankind: Equal Employment Opportunities for women!

U.S.A., 1970

Equal Pay for Women - at long last!

G.B., 1978

Financial equality at last: wives are to receive their own tax rebates!

4

William Congreve

"Battle of the Sexes"*

The following scene has been taken from act IV of William Congreve's play *The Way of the World* (first performed in 1700), one of the greatest English comedies of manners of the Restoration period. Mirabell and Mrs Millamant, the hero and heroine of the play, have finally decided to get married. – *Six Restoration Plays*, ed. by John Harold Wilson (Cambridge, Mass.: The Riverside Press, 1959), pp. 366-368.

MIRABELL "Like Daphne she, as lovely and as coy". Do you lock yourself up from me to make my search more curious, or is this pretty artifice contrived to signify that here the chase must end, and my pursuit be crowned? For you can fly no further.

MILLAMANT Vanity! No – I'll fly and be followed to the last moment. Though I am upon the very verge of matrimony, I expect you should solicit me as much as if I were wavering at the grate of a monastery, with one foot over the threshold. I'll be solicited to the very last – nay, and afterwards.

MIRABELL What, after the last?

MILLAMANT Oh, I should think I was poor and had nothing to bestow, if I were reduced to an inglorious ease and freed from the agreeable fatigues of solicitation.

MIRABELL But do you not know that when favors are conferred upon instant and tedious solicitation, that they diminish in their value, and that both the giver loses the grace, and the receiver lessens his pleasure?

MILLAMANT It may be in things of common application; but never, sure, in love. Oh, I hate a lover that can dare to think he draws a moment's air, independent of the bounty of his mistress. There is not so impudent a thing in nature as the saucy look of an assured man, confident of success. The pedantic arrogance of a very husband has not so pragmatical an air. Ah! I'll never marry unless I am first made sure of my will and pleasure.

MIRABELL Would you have 'em both before marriage? or will you be contented with the first now, and stay for the other till after grace?

MILLAMANT Ah! Don't be impertinent. – My dear liberty, shall I leave thee? my faithful solitude, my darling contemplation, must I bid you then adieu? Ay–h adieu – my morning thoughts, agreeable wakings, indolent slumbers, all ye douceurs, ye sommeils du matin, adieu.

– I can't do't, 'tis more than impossible. – Positively, Mirabell, I'll lie abed in a morning as long as I please.

MIRABELL Then I'll get up in a morning as early as I please.

MILLAMANT Ah? Idle creature, get up when you will – and d'ye hear, I won't be called names after I'm married; positively, I won't be called names.

MIRABELL Names!

MILLAMANT Aye, as wife, spouse, my dear, joy, jewel, love, sweetheart, and the rest of that nauseous cant, in which men and their wives are so fulsomely familiar – I shall never bear that. Good Mirabell, don't let us be familiar or fond, nor kiss before folks, like ...; nor go to Hyde Park together the first Sunday in a new chariot, to provoke eyes and whispers, and then never be seen there together again, as if we were proud of one another the first week, and ashamed of one another ever after. Let us never visit together, nor go to a play together; but let us be very strange and well-bred. Let us be as strange as if we had been married a great while, and as well-bred as if we were not married at all.

MIRABELL Have you any more conditions to offer? Hitherto your demands are pretty reasonable.

MILLAMANT Trifles – as liberty to pay and receive visits to and from whom I please; to write and receive letters, without interrogatories or wry faces on your part; to wear what I please, and choose conversation with regard only to my own taste; to have no obligation upon me to converse with wits that I don't like, because they are your acquaintance; or to be intimate with fools, because they may be your relations. Come to dinner when I please; dine in my dressing-room when I'm out of humor, without giving a reason. To have my closet inviolate, to be sole empress of my tea-table, which you must never presume to approach without first asking leave. And lastly, wherever I am, you shall always knock at the door before you come in. These articles subscribed, if I continue to endure you a little longer, I may by degrees dwindle into a wife.

MIRABELL Your bill of fare is something advanced in this latter account. Well, have I liberty to offer conditions – that when you are dwindled into a wife, I may not be beyond measure enlarged into a husband?

MILLAMANT You have free leave. Propose your utmost; speak and spare not.

MIRABELL I thank you. – Imprimis then, I covenant that your acquaintance be general; that you admit no sworn confidante or intimate of your own sex – no she-friend to screen her affairs under your countenance, and tempt you to make trial of a mutual secrecy. No decoy-duck to wheedle you a fop-scrambling to the play in a mask, then bring you home in a pretended fright, when you think you shall be found out, and rail at me for missing the play and disappointing the frolic which you had, to pick me up and prove my constancy.

MILLAMANT Detestable imprimis! I go to the play in a mask!

MIRABELL Item, I article that you continue to like your own face as long as I shall; and while it passes current with me, that you endeavour not to new-coin it. To which end, together with all vizards for the day, I prohibit all masks for the night, made of oiled-skins and I know not what – hog's bones, hare's gall, pig-water, and the marrow of a roasted cat. In short, I forbid all commerce with the gentlewoman in what-d'ye-call-it Court. Item, I shut my doors against all bawds with basket, and pennyworths of muslin, china, fans, atlases, etc. – Item, when you shall be breeding –

MILLAMANT Ah! name it not.

MIRABELL Which may be presumed, with a blessing on our endeavours –

MILLAMANT Odious endeavours!

MIRABELL I denounce against all strait lacing, squeezing for a shape, till you mould my boy's head to a sugar-loaf, and instead of a man-child, make me father to a crooked billet. Lastly, to the dominion of the tea-table I submit, but with proviso, that you exceed not in your province, but restrain yourself to native and simple tea-table drinks, as tea, chocolate, and coffee; as likewise to genuine and authorized tea-table talk – such as mending of fashions, spoiling reputations, railing at absent friends, and so forth – but that on no account you encroach upon the men's prerogative, and presume to drink healths, or toast fellows; for prevention of which I banish all foreign forces, all auxiliaries to the tea-table, as orange-brandy, all aniseed, cinnamon, citron, and Barbados waters, together with ratafia, and the most noble spirit of clary, but for cowslip wine, poppy water, and all dormitives, those I allow. These provisos admitted, in other things I may prove a tractable and complying husband.

MILLAMANT O horrid provisos! filthy strong-waters! I toast fellows! odious men! I hate your odious provisos.

MIRABELL Then we're agreed. Shall I kiss your hand upon the contract?

William Congreve (1670-1729) was one of the most renowned Restoration dramatists. He was born in Bardsey, Yorkshire, spent his childhood in Ireland, and became a student at Trinity College, Dublin. In 1691, he studied law in London. His first publications were verse and a novel, but he won fame with his first comedy, *The Old Bachelor*, in 1693. A succession of other comedies, and one tragedy, followed. His works were censured by Jeremy Collier, a clergyman and author of *A Short View of the Immorality and Profaneness of the English Stage* (1698), since when Restoration Comedy has been labelled as licentious. Congreve's famous comedy, *The Way of the World*, was coolly received in 1700. Congreve held government sinecures, enjoyed the friendship and admiration of Swift, Steele, Pope, and was intimately attached to the Duchess of Marlborough. In 1726 he was visited by Voltaire. Congreve is buried in Westminster Abbey.

Info

Restoration

It was the period in Britain following the return of Charles II as king on May 29, 1660, which turned London from the austerities of puritanism to the pursuit of pleasure. The period was characterized by advances in trade, opposition to the Roman Catholic religion, the establishment of the Whig and Tory political parties, and new developments in poetry and the theatre. After the re-opening of theatres, the King licensed two companies: The King's Company and the Duke's Company. Soon after their founding, both companies began to employ actresses. Thus, for the first time in the history of the English stage, women played the female roles formerly entrusted to boys. This daring innovation, while adding to the theatrical illusion of reality, had an unfortunate effect on the development of the new drama. Many of the actresses, who were underpaid, became demi-mondaines (i.e. women of questionable reputation) and playwrights were quick to capitalize upon their demi-reputations by writing provocative, erotic roles for them. A good share of the emphasis upon sex and sensuality in Restoration drama resulted from the introduction of women on the stage.

Vocabulary

1 coy (adj.): modest, shy - **3 curious** (adj.): difficult, elaborate, careful - **3 artifice** (n.): device, contrivance, skill - **3 to contrive** (v.): to invent - **4 chase** (n.): pursuit - **5 to fly** (v.): here to run away, to flee - **7 on the verge of**: very near to - **8 matrimony** (v.): formal for the state of being married - **8 to solicit** (v.): to invite, to make appeals or requests to - **9 grate** (n.): frame of metal bars for confining s.th. or s.o. - **11 nay** (adv.): old use for no - **14 to bestow** (v.): formal for to give - **14 inglorious** (adj.): literary for shameful, bringing dishonour - **18 to confer upon** (v.): formal for to give (a title, honour, favour, etc.) - **18 instant** (adj.): urgent - **18 tedious** (adj.): boring - **20 grace** (n.): willingness to behave in a fair and honourable way - **21f. application** (n.): the act of putting s.th. to use - **24 bounty** (n.): esp. literary for generosity - **24 impudent** (adj.): rude and disrespectful, esp. to an older or more important person - **25 saucy** (adj.): producing sexual interest in an amusing way - **27 pragmatical** (adj.): conceited - **32 grace** (n.): here after the marriage vows - **33 impertinent** (adj.): rude and disrespectful - **35 to bid s.o. adieu**: /a'dju:/ literary for to say good-bye - **36 indolent** (v.): formal for lazy - **37 ye** (pron.): old use for you - **37 douceurs** (n.): pleasures - **37 sommeils du matin**: day-dreams - **39 abed** (adj.): old use for in bed - **43 to call s.o. names**: to abuse or insult s.o. - **46 aye** (adv.): /aɪ/ dialect or literary for yes - **46 spouse** (n.): formal or law for a husband or wife - **47 nauseous** (adj.): /nɔːziəs/ detestable; here: the word is not used with the strong emphasis it has today - **48 cant** (n.): /kænt/ derogatory for insincere talk - **48 fulsomely** (adv.): effusively - **50 fond** (adj.): foolishly loving - **52 chariot** (n.): a light-four-wheeled carriage - **52 eyes** (n.): here: interest, curiosity - **56 well-bred** (adj.): old-fashioned for having good manners - **60 hitherto** (adv.): formal for up until now - **61 trifle** (n.): a matter of slight importance - **63 interrogatories** (n.): questions - **63 wry** (adj.): showing a mixture of amusement and displeasure - **66 wit** (n.): a person who has the ability to say things which are both clever and amusing - **69 out of humor**: old-fashioned formal for in a bad temper - **70 closet** (n.): a cupboard built into the wall of a room - **70 inviolate** (adj.): literary for not broken into - **71 empress** (n.): a female emperor, here ruler - **72 to presume** (v.): here:

Info

Marriage

was a favourite topic with the Restoration dramatists, and frequently it is the main butt [i.e. target] of their satire. To understand why, it is necessary to remember what marriage involved in seventeenth-century England. Marriage was not then a private and wholly voluntary contract between two individuals. As in many parts of the world today, it was felt to be the concern of the family group. Matches were generally arranged by the heads of families, by fathers or elder brothers. An entry in Samuel Pepys's diary concerning his brother's marriage illustrates the typical attitude fairly well: "My chiefest thought is now to get a good wife for Tom, there being one offered by the Joyces, a cozen of theirs, worth £200 in ready money." (31 December 1661)

Among the wealthy classes such matters as fixing a dowry and jointure and preserving or enlarging family estates took priority. The wishes of those about to be married were not entirely ignored, but normally had to take second place. Women seldom had much say in the choice of their partners. Traditionally they were conceded the right to refuse a proposed husband, but refusal might well involve a more then average degree of heroism. Men were allowed greater freedom of choice, but would rarely risk offending relatives on whom they depended financially. Parents still occasionally arranged marriages between young children in this period; young women were sometimes coupled with middle-aged men [...].

P.F. Vernon, William Wycherley *(Harlow: Longman, 1965), pp. 10f.*

formal for to behave without enough respect or politeness - **72f. to ask leave**: formal for to ask permission - **74 article** (n.): a complete separate part in a legal agreement, etc. - **74f. to subscribe** (v.): formal for to sign - **76 to dwindle** (v.): to become steadily fewer or smaller - **77 bill of fare**: menu - **78 account** (n.): old use for counting, calculation - **80 beyond measure**: more than what is necessary - **82 utmost** (n.): esp. literary for the most that can be done - **82 to spare** (v.): to refrain from hurting, damaging or destroying - **83 imprimis** (adv.): in the first place; a term used in legal contracts - **83 to covenant** (v.): to promise in writing - **85 sworn** (adj.): complete and with no possibility of changing - **85 confidante** (n.): a person, here female, to whom one tells one's secrets or with whom one talks about personal matters - **86 countenance** (n.): support or approval - **87 trial** (n.): testing, trying, proving - **87 mutual** (adj.): equally shared by each one - **87 secrecy** (n.): the practice of keeping secrets - **87f. decoy-duck** (n.): here a person or thing used to tempt s.b. into a position of danger - **89 mask** (n.): cover for the upper part of the face, made of silk or velvet - **90 to rail at** (v.): formal for to express angry disapproval or complaint - **91 frolic** (n.): an active and enjoyable game of amusement - **92 constancy** (n.): faithfulness, loyalty - **95 item** (adv.): formal, esp. old use for and in addition, also - **95 to article** (v.): to formulate in articles, to make stipulations - **96f. to pass current**: to be generally accepted as true or genuine - **97 to new-coin** (v.): here to change - **98 vizard** (n.): mask - **102 commerce** (n.): the buying and selling of goods and services - **103 bawd** (n.): old use or literary for a woman who keeps a house of prostitutes - **104 pennyworth** (n.): BrE formal for bargain - **104 muslin** (n.): very fine thin cotton cloth - **104 china** (n.): a hard white substance made by baking fine clay at high temperatures - **104 fan** (n.): an instrument for making a flow of air - **104 atlas** (n.): silk satin manu-factured in the Orient, flowered with gold or silver - **105 breeding** (n.): being pregnant - **107 blessing** (n.): an act of asking or receiving God's favour, help, or protection - **108 endeavour** (n.): formal or pompous for effort - **109 odious** (adj.): formal for very unpleasant - **110 to denounce** (v.): to express strong disapproval of - **110 strait lacing** (n.): tightly laced corsets - **110f. squeezing** (n.): an act of pressing in from opposite sides or around - **111 to mould** (v.): to fit closely to the shape of s.th., esp. a body - **111f. sugar-loaf** (n.): conical moulded mass of sugar - **112 man-child** (n.): a male child - **113 crooked billet** (n.): a bent stick - **114 proviso** (n.): necessary condition in an agreement that is made in advance - **114 to exceed** (v.): derogatory for to do more than (what is legal, necessary, etc.) - **115 province** (n.): an area of knowledge, activity, etc., esp. one that is regarded as belonging to a particular person - **115 to restrain** (v.): here to restrict o.s. to - **115 native** (adj.): here unadorned, simple, artless - **116 likewise** (adv.): formal for in the same way, similarly - **119f. to encroach upon** (v.): to take more than is right, usual, or acceptable - **120 prerogative** (n.): a special right belonging to a particular person - **120 to drink s.o.'s health**: (before drinking) a wish for s.o.'s success and continued freedom from illness - **121 to toast** (v.): to drink in a ceremonial way in order to express good wishes to s.o. - **122 auxiliary** (n.): formal for a helper or assistant - **122f. orange-brandy** (n.): brandy flavoured with orange peel - **123ff. aniseed ... ratafia** (n.): all these drinks were made of brandy, variously flavoured - **125 clary** (n.): a drink made from brandy and clary flowers with the addition of sugar, cinnamon, etc. - **125 cowslip wine** (n.): wine made from a small European wild plant of the primrose family - **125 poppy** (n.): a plant that has brightly coloured flowers, esp. red ones - **126 dormitive** (n.): drink to induce sleep - **127 tractable** (n.): formal for easily controlled - **127 complying** (adj.): formal for acting in accordance with a demand, rule, etc. - **129 filthy** (adj.): dirty, immoral - **129 strong-water** (n.): a strong alcoholic drink

Explanations

12 "What, after the last?": The proviso scene allows for a wide, lightly satirical survey of follies, affectations, and deceptions by partners in a marriage - **88 to wheedle you a fop-scrambling to the play**: to lure you to the theatre to compete for the company of a foolish man; a fop is one of the humorous character types in Restoration comedy, opposed to the rational type of a wit - **99ff. oiled-skins, hog's bones, hare's gall, pig-water and the marrow of roasted cat**: all of these were ingredients in cosmetics - **102 the gentlewoman in what-d'ye-call-it Court**: an unexplained topical reference - **129 filthy**: like 'nauseous', the word is not used with the strong emphasis it has today.

Awareness

1 An increasing number of people intending to get married nowadays agree on a marriage contract. What could be the motivation behind it? Do you understand their motivation?

Comprehension

2 What is meant by "pursuit" (l. 4) in the context of the scene?
3 How does Mirabell try to dissuade Millamant from continually evading him?
4 What is Millamant's idea of the relationship between lovers (ll. 8-29)?
5 What is her concept of liberty?
6 Why does she want her relationship with Mirabell to be different?
7 This is an excerpt from the famous proviso scene of *The Way of the World*. What does the term "proviso" (see l. 114) mean in the context of this scene?
8 Make lists of the conditions Mrs Millamant and Mirabell each put forward for the marriage contract.

Analysis

9 Compare the two lists in exercise 8 and explain what they reveal about aristocratic men and women at the time of the Restoration.
10 Find out elements in the text which describe a typical day in the life of Mrs Millamant.
11 When you read the text for the first time, it must seem rather unfamiliar because it contains a lot of contemporary cultural information. Go through the text again and find out characteristic habits (linguistic, medicinal, cultural).
12 Restoration aristocrats prided themselves on their clever use of rhetoric. Analyse characteristic stylistic devices which may prove this point.

Opinion

13 Compare our way of life with that of Restoration aristocrats.
14 Comment on the English proverb "Familiarity breeds contempt" in view of this proviso scene.
15 Imagine you are a clairvoyant. Look into your crystal ball and predict whether the marriage between Mrs Millamant and Mirabell will be successful.
16 Would you say that this is a classic example of the "battle of the sexes"?

Project

17 Make a survey of the different marriage rites and customs in G.B., the U.S.A. and your own country. *The Dictionary of English Language and Culture* (Harlow: Longman, 1992) could give you some ideas. Try to find out about some of the legal aspects as well.

Suggested Further Reading

18 Read O.F. Morshead (ed.), *The Diary of Samuel Pepys* (London: Bell and Sons, 1927) and Rose Tremain, *Restoration* (London: Sceptre, 1990) to give you a more detailed idea of the historical period.

5

"It is a truth universally acknowledged ...": Jane Austen and the Marriage Market

For a long period of time the English novelist Jane Austen (1775 - 1817) had a small, but devoted following among academics, especially those who were interested in gender studies. In recent years there has been a Jane Austen "boom", which began with the first BBC film production of her novel *Pride and Prejudice* (first published in 1813); it has resulted in a number of film versions of her other novels and culminated in the recent new film version of *Pride and Prejudice* starring Keira Knightley, Judi Dench and Donald Sutherland, which had its German film debut in October 2005. The topic of young women of the landed gentry on the lookout for a husband, competing against each other in the process, seems rather old-fashioned, but the motivations and machinations of the literary characters have fascinated recent audiences and readers. - Jane Austen, *Pride and Prejudice* (Harmondsworth: Penguin, 1972).

Mr and Mrs Bennet with their five daughters

Plot Outline

"It is a truth universally acknowledged, that a single man in possession of a good fortune must be in want of a wife." The famous beginning of *Pride and Prejudice* is a truism which immediately plunges the reader into the marriage market of the novel. The problem arises from the necessity of attracting a likely candidate in the proper way or, failing that, in a way which may be taken to be proper by society. However, the problem becomes even more acute, if one looks at the disproportionate distribution of participants: 9 marrigeable young women are confronted with 4, more or less, eligible men. This shortage among the male domain makes it apparent to the reader/viewer how cruel the mechanisms of the market can be to any individual, whose personal likes and dislikes are hardly ever considered. A group of busybodies participating in the market are mothers like Mrs Bennet whose sole interest it is to have her five daughters married.

The following excerpt deals with the first proposal of Mr Darcy, a highly eligible man from Derbyshire, whose declaration of love seems rather offensive to Elizabeth Bennet, the second of the Bennet daughters and the most sensible one. Her rejection of the proposal does not only come as a shock to the suitor, but puts herself, from the market point of view, into a dicey situation, since she must fear to be left on the shelf owing to a lack of candidates.

To understand the strained atmosphere and Elizabeth's rejection of Darcy it is necessary to review what has preceded this escalation. On his arrival at the marriage market of Meryton, Darcy is seen as a likely candidate for one of the eligible daughters, but since he refuses to play the game, public opinion turns against him and he is declared to be proud and distant.

In this episode Elizabeth still shares the prejudices of her social group, which is enhanced by the fact that at their first meeting Darcy offends her by refusing to dance with her, as "'She is tolerable, but not handsome enough to tempt [him].'"Elizabeth is determined to hate him.

As the plot develops, they are in each other's company for considerable lengths of time, which causes Darcy to mellow and to see some redeeming features in her intelligence and playfulness. Elizabeth, however, perceives everything about him in such a way that the prejudices she holds against him can only deepen. When she finds out that Darcy has discouraged his friend Bingley from being involved with Elizabeth's eldest sister Jane, she condemns him completely. Her dislike reaches its highest point, whereas Darcy cannot resist her charms and makes her an offer of marriage against his better judgement.

A strained visit to Netherfield Park: Mr Bingley, his elegant sister Caroline and Mr Darcy are pretending to welcome female members of the Bennet family, while Elizabeth (on the left) is hoping not to be embarrassed by her relatives.

After a silence of several minutes he came towards her in an agitated manner and thus began.

'In vain have I struggled. It will not do. My feelings will not be repressed. You must allow me to tell you how ardently I admire and love you.'

Elizabeth's astonishment was beyond expression. She stared, coloured, doubted, and was silent. This he considered sufficient encouragement, and the avowal of all that he felt and had long felt for her, immediately followed. He spoke well, but there were feelings besides those of the heart to be detailed, and he was not more eloquent on the subject of tenderness than of pride. His sense of her inferiority - of its being a degradation - of the family obstacles which judgment had always opposed to inclination, were dwelt on with a warmth which seemed due to the consequence he was wounding, but was very unlikely to recommend his suit.

In spite of her deeply-rooted dislike, she could not be insensible to the compliment of such a man's affection, and though her intentions did not vary for an instant, she was at first sorry for the pain he was to receive; till, roused to resentment by his subsequent language, she lost all compassion in anger. She tried, however, to compose herself to answer him with patience, when he should have done. He concluded with representing to her the strength of that attachment which, in spite of all his endeavours, he had found impossible to conquer; and with expressing his hope that it would now be rewarded by her acceptance of his hand. As he said this, she could easily see that he had no doubt of a favourable answer. He spoke of apprehension and anxiety, but his countenance expressed real security. Such a circumstance could only exasperate farther, and when he ceased, the colour rose into her cheeks, and she said,

'In such cases as this, it is, I believe, the established mode to express a sense of obligation for the sentiments avowed, however unequally they may be returned. It is natural that obligation should be felt, and if I could feel gratitude, I would now thank you. But I cannot - I have never desired your good opinion, and you have certainly bestowed it most unwillingly. I am sorry to have occasioned pain to any one. It has been most unconsciously done, however, and I hope will be of short duration. The feelings which, you tell me, have long prevented the acknowledgment of your regard, can have little difficulty in overcoming it after this explanation.'

Mr Darcy, who was leaning against the mantle-piece with his eyes fixed on her face, seemed to catch her words with no less resentment than surprise. His complexion became pale with anger, and the disturbance of his mind was visible in every feature. He was struggling for the appearance of composure, and would not open his lips, till he believed himself to have attained it. The pause was to Elizabeth's feelings dreadful. At length, in a voice of forced calmness he said,

'And this is all the reply I have the honour of expecting! I might, perhaps, wish to be informed why, with so little endeavour at civility, I am thus rejected. But it is of small importance.'

'I might as well enquire,' replied she, 'why with so evident a design of offending and insulting me, you chose to tell me that you liked me against your will, against your reason, and even against your character? Was not this some excuse for incivility, if I was uncivil? [...]'

Basildon Park, one of the locations for the 2005 film version of Pride and Prejudice

Jane Austen (1775-1817) was the daughter of a Hampshire clergyman. She always loved reading and started writing stories and burlesque novels at an early age. The first of her novels to be published was *Sense and Sensibility* (1811). Although Jane Austen led a very quiet life and never got married, her descriptions of contemporary society and of the relationships between women and men even today are widely acclaimed and loved by readers all over the world.

Vocabulary

Intro: machinations (pl. n.): secret, clever, and often unfair methods used to achieve s.th. - **1 acknowledge** (v.): to admit or accept that s.th. is true - **2 fortune** (n.): a very large amount of money - **4 truism** (n.): statement that is clearly true - **9 acute** (adj.): very serious - **12 eligible** (adj.): good to marry - **25 suitor** (n.) (old use): a man who wants to marry a particular woman - **27 dicey** (adj.): slightly dangerous and uncertain - **59 ardent** (adj./lit.): showing strong feelings of love - **61 colour** (v./lit.): when s.o. colours, their face becomes redder because they are embarrassed - **62 avowal** (n.): /ə'vaʊəl/ a public statement about s.th. you believe in - **65 detail** (v.): to list things or give all the facts or information about s.th. - **67 degradation** (n.): here: change from a higher to a lower moral and social standard - **70 consequence** (n.): here: social importance - **76 resentment** (n.): a feeling of anger because s.th. has happened that you think is unfair - **76 subsequent** (adj.) happening or coming after s.th. else - **81 endeavour** (n.):

an attempt to do s.th. new or difficult - **85f. countenance** (n.): your face or your expression - **87 exasperate** (v.): to make s.o. very annoyed by continuing to do s.th. that upsets them - **90 obligation** (n.): a moral or legal duty to do s.th. - **95 bestow** (v.): to give s.o. s.th. of great value or importance - **96 occasion** (v.): to cause s.th. - **101 mantlepiece** (n.): (mod. BrE: mantelpiece) a wooden or stone shelf which is the top part of a frame surrounding a fireplace - **106 composure** (n.) the state of feeling or seeming calm - **112 civility** (n.) polite behaviour which most people consider normal

Awareness

1 A proverb says that marriages are made in heaven. Imagine that your dream partner "pops the question". What would the ambience be like? What would the wording of the proposal be?

2 Where in a person's life is etiquette of significance even in our modern world?

Comprehension

3 What compliments does Darcy verbalise?

4 In addition to the positive aspects he mentions what are his reservations about the match?

5 How does Elizabeth react

a) to the situation in general

b) to his mention of reservations?

6 Why does her reaction take Darcy by surprise?

7 How does the conversation end?

Analysis

8 Analyse the choice of words and the tone in which the conversation takes place.

9 Make lists of positive and negative terms to describe appropriate and inappropriate social behaviour.

10 Analyse the non-verbial behaviour of both interlocutors.

Projects

11 Find out about life in Georgian England: in particular how society was structured, how marriages were arranged, what concept of etiquette prevailed, what social mobility meant for men and for women. You might find lots of hints about the facts of daily life in 19th-century England in the novels of Jane Austen herself and in Daniel Pool's *What Jane Austen ATE and Charles Dickens KNEW* (New York: 1993).

12 Design a film version of this episode.

Internet Projects

13 Check www.imdb.com and find out about the number and variety of film versions of Jane Austen's *Pride and Prejudice.* How can the attraction the material and plot still have on modern viewers be explained?

14 Choose two film versions and compare

a) how characters and setting are rendered

b) the cinematographic devices the producer uses. For ideas check the film glossary (pp. 49-55) in: *Viewfinder Topics Film, Soap and Photo* by D. Düwel and J. von der Grün.

Further Reading

15 Read the book that would have been more valuable to Mrs Bennet and at least one of her daughters than any book of etiquette: Rachel Greenwald, *The Program: How to Find a Husband After Thirty* (London: Timewarner 2004). According to the British newspaper *The Observer* this book is "the hottest thing to hit the dating scene since *Sex and the City*". The author uses not only the strategies but also the market technology she learned at Harvard Business School and turns the search for a husband into a business transaction. This is a modern version of the marriage market at the time of Jane Austen.

16 Read Karen Joy Fowler's novel *The Jane Austen Book Club* (London: Penguin 2004), which begins with the truism "Each of us has a private Jane Austen" (p. 1).

17 Read the following sequels to *Pride and Prejudice:*
Pemberley by Emma Tenant (London: Hodder and Stoughton, 1993)
Presumption by Julia Barrett (New York, 1993)
An Unequal Marriage or Pride and Prejudice Twenty Years Later by Emma Tennant (New York: St. Martin's Press, 1994)

6

Kate Chopin

"The Story of an Hour"

Kate Chopin is known to be a pioneer in the treatment of sexuality in American literature, discussing woman's desire to become a person in her own right. In "The Story of an Hour" she shows how an hour can change a woman's life. – *The Complete Works of Kate Chopin*, ed. by Peer Seyerstedt (Baton Rouge: Louisiana State University Press, 1966), pp. 352-357.

Knowing that Mrs. Mallard was afflicted with a heart trouble, great care was taken to break to her as gently as possible the news of her husband's death.

It was her sister Josephine who told her, in broken sentences, veiled hints that revealed in half concealing. Her husband's friend Richards was there, too, near her. It was he who had been in the newspaper office when intelligence of the railroad disaster was received, with Brently Mallard's name leading the list of "killed." He had only taken the time to assure himself of its truth by a second telegram, and had hastened to forestall any less careful, less tender friend in bearing the sad message.

She did not hear the story as many women have heard the same, with a paralyzed inability to accept its significance. She wept at once, with sudden, wild abandonment, in her sister's arms. When the storm of grief had spent itself she went away to her room alone. She would have no one follow her.

There stood, facing the window, a comfortable, roomy armchair. Into this she sank, pressed down by a physical exhaustion that haunted her body and seemed to reach into her soul.

She could see in the open square before her house the tops of trees that were all aquiver with the new spring life. The delicious breath of rain was in the air. In the street below a peddler was crying his wares. The notes of a distant song which someone was singing reached her faintly, and countless sparrows were twittering in the eaves.

There were patches of blue sky showing here and there through the clouds that had met and piled above the other in the west facing her window.

She sat with her head thrown back upon the cushion of the chair quite motionless, except when a sob came up into her throat and shook her, as a child who has cried itself to sleep continues to sob in its dreams.

She was young, with a fair, calm face, whose lines bespoke repression and even a certain strength. But now there was a dull stare in her eyes, whose gaze was fixed away off yonder on one of those patches of blue sky. It was not a glance of reflection, but rather indicated a suspension of intelligent thought.

There was something coming to her and she was for it, fearfully.

What was it? She did not know; it was too subtle and elusive to name. But she felt it, creeping out of the sky, reaching toward her through the sounds, the scents, the color that filled the air.

Now her bosom rose and fell tumultuously. She was beginning to recognize this thing that was approaching to possess her, and she was striving to beat it back with her will – as powerless as her two white slender hands would have been.

When she abandoned herself a little whispered word escaped her slightly parted lips. She said it over and over under her breath: "Free, free, free!" The vacant stare and the look of terror that had followed it went from her eyes. They stayed keen and bright. Her pulses beat fast, and the coursing blood warmed and relaxed every inch of her body.

She did not stop to ask if it were not a monstrous joy that held her. A clear and exalted perception enabled her to dismiss the suggestion as trivial.

She knew that she would weep again when she saw the kind, tender hands folded in death; the face that had never looked save with love upon her, fixed and gray and dead. But she saw beyond that bitter moment a long procession of years to come that would belong to her absolutely. And she opened and spread her arms out to them in welcome.

There would be no one to live for during those coming years; she would live for herself. There would be no powerful will bending her in that blind persistence with which men and women believe they have a right to impose a private will upon a fellow-creature. A kind intention or a cruel intention made the act seem no less a crime as she looked upon it in that brief moment of illumination.

And yet she had loved him – sometimes. Often she had not. What did it matter! What could love, the unsolved mystery, count for in face of this possession of self-assertion which she suddenly recognized as the strongest impulse of her being!

"Free! Body and soul free!" she kept whispering.

Josephine was kneeling before the closed door with her lips to the keyhole, imploring admission. "Louise, open the door! I beg; open the door – you will make yourself ill. What are you doing, Louise? For heaven's sake open the door."

"Go away. I am not making myself ill." No; she was drinking in a very elixir of life through that open window.

Her fancy was running riot along those days ahead of her. Spring days, and summer days, and all sorts of days that would be her own. She breathed a quick prayer that life might be long.

She arose at length and opened the door to her sister's importunities. There was a feverish triumph in her eyes, and she carried herself unwittingly like a goddess of Victory. She clasped her sister's waist, and together they descended the stairs. Richards stood waiting for them at the bottom.

Some one was opening the front door with a latchkey. It was Brently Mallard who entered, a little travel-stained, composedly carrying his gripsack and umbrella. He had been far from the scene of the accident, and did not even know there had been one. He stood amazed at Josephine's piercing cry; at Richards' quick motion to screen him from the view of his wife.

But Richards was too late.

When the doctors came they said that she had died of heart disease – of joy that kills.

Kate Chopin (1851-1904) was born Katherine O'Flaherty in St. Louis, the daughter of an Irish merchant and a French-Creole mother. In 1870, she married Oscar Chopin (the name is pronounced like the composer's), who took her off to Europe on their honeymoon during which she made the acquaintance of Victoria Woodhull, an outspoken advocate of women's rights, birth control, and free love, who warned her of the entrapment marriage could bring. From Kate Chopin a line can be drawn to the Seneca Falls Convention (see pp. 11ff.), because she knew most of the women involved in the movement. When her husband had died of swamp fever in 1882, she was left with six children to bring up. After she had paid off his debts, she returned to St. Louis and began to write, predominantly short stories. Her novel *The Awakening* was published in 1899 and was considered to be scandalous because of its sexual frankness. Though her work was neglected at first, she has attracted a lot of interest from feminist scholars, who see her as a pioneer of the new sexuality.

Info

Objective correlative

A term first used by T.S. Eliot to describe a pattern of objects, actions, or events, or a situation which can serve effectively to awaken in the reader the emotional response which the author desires without being a direct statement of that emotion. It is an impersonal or objective means of communicating feeling. Eliot calls the objective correlative "the only way of expressing emotion in the form of art" and defines it as "a set of objects, a situation, a chain of events which shall be the formula of that particular emotion, such that when the external facts, which must terminate in sensory experience, are given, the emotion is immediately evoked." The term has had wide currency in this sense among contemporary critics.

A Handbook to Literature, *ed. by C. Hugh Holman (Indiana: Bobbs-Merrill, 1975), pp. 361f.*

Vocabulary

1 to be afflicted (v.): to suffer in the body or mind - **8 intelligence** (n.): here news - **11 to forestall** (v.): to prevent by taking action first - **16 abandonment** (n.): giving o.s. completely to an emotion - **16f. the storm had spent itself**: the storm had died down - **21 to haunt** (v.): here to take over - **24 aquiver** (adj.): in a state of vibrant agitation - **26 peddler** (n.): (AmE) person who sells small articles in the street - **28 sparrow** (n.): a small brownish bird, very common in some parts of the world - **29 eaves** (n.): overhanging edges of the roof - **34 sob** (n.): an act of making short bursts of sound as one breathes in, because of sadness or fear - **38 to bespeak** (v.): formal for to indicate, to be evidence of - **40 yonder** (adv.): old use or dialect for over there - **42 suspension** (n.): stopping or causing to be inactive or ineffective for a period of time - **46 elusive** (adj.): hard to grasp - **56 under one's breath**: in a whisper - **62 exalted** (adj.): /ɪg'zɔːltɪd/ high, noble - **66 save** (conj.): except - **73 persistence** (n.): the act of continuing steadily in some course of action - **81f. self-assertion** (n.): the putting forward of one's own claims in a determined manner - **92 to run riot** (v.): to throw off all discipline - **97 importunity** (n.): persistent request - **98 unwittingly** (adv.): not knowing or not intended - **102 latchkey** (n.): the key to an outer door - **104 gripsack** (n.): holdall, large bag - **107 piercing** (adj.): sharp

Explanations

Biography Kate Chopin/French-Creole: a white person descended from the original French settlers in the Southern U.S. Chopin's tales are set among the Creoles and Acadians in Louisiana and help establish the author as a leading exponent of the local-color school.

Awareness

1 Throughout history people have entered into marital relationships. List some of the reasons that may have motivated them to get married, in the past and also today.
2 About one in three marriages ends in divorce (in the U.S., almost one in two). In view of that fact, why do you think that the majority of people still get married?
3 Some people believe that an hour can change a person's entire life. – List arguments in favor of and against this statement.

Comprehension

4 What news has to be broken to Mrs Mallard?
5 Where does Richards have the information from?
6 Who is Richards?
7 What are Mrs Mallard's reactions to the news?
8 What are her plans for the future?
9 Why is love an "unsolved mystery" (ll. 80f.) for Mrs Mallard?
10 What happens when she goes downstairs?
11 What is the doctors' explanation for Mrs Mallard's unexpected death?

Analysis

12 Relate the title to the plot of the story.
13 Characterize Mrs Mallard.
14 Go through the text again and analyse how suspense is created in the story.
15 In narrative fiction the description of nature frequently functions as an objective correlative (see p. 27). Analyse the description of nature in this story and what it suggests.
16 Analyse the structure of the story, especially in relation to its beginning and its ending.

Opinion

17 The reader is most probably amazed at two facts: Mr Mallard was a kind husband and Mrs Mallard even loved him (sometimes). Do you think that her reaction to the news of her husband's death is plausible? Give reasons for your opinion.
18 In view of the facts on the Seneca Falls Convention (text 3) and the women involved in it, discuss whether Mrs Mallard can be considered a true woman of her times.

Projects

19 Re-write the passage of the story in which nature is described (ll. 23-32) from the point of view of a true mourner.
20 Mr and Mrs Mallard consult a marriage guidance counsellor. In groups of three, carry out the counselling interview and speculate on what advice the counsellor will give them. Then re-write the ending of the short story accordingly.
21 Re-write the story from Brently Mallard's point of view.
22 Write out the two telegrams which arrive at the newspaper office (to be read by Mr Richards).

Info

Feminism

The advocacy of the rights and equality of women in social, political, and economic spheres, and a commitment to the fundamental alteration of woman's role in society. Precursors of the formal movement range from Aristophanes' Lysistrata to 19th century novelists such as Charlotte Brontë. Early feminist campaigners like Mrs Emmeline Pankhurst concentrated upon the political aspects of female subjugation, with female suffrage as their principal end; subsequently the emphasis shifted to economic and social equality in the form of equal pay and equal opportunity. New methods of birth control and a changing climate of public opinion have enabled the women's movement to score some successes in the area of legislation, and a more widespread acceptance of equality in education, work, and the home. Both the aims and the image of the feminist movement have, however, altered with the advent of Women's Liberation as an activist and militant wing whose more radical elements insist that the entire social system is pervaded by a sexism which structures and maintains oppression in psychological and biological terms. The type of feminism which sees women as possessing uniquely feminine qualities and abilities and wishes to see such qualities reflected in social roles, is now attacked and undermined by this vanguard of Women's Liberation.

The Fontana Dictionary of Modern Thought *(London: Fontana, 1977), p. 231*

7

William Brandon

"The Wild Freedom of the Mountain Men"

The following is an excerpt from William Brandon's book *The Men and the Mountain,* in which he gives an account of an expedition to the West in 1848 which was carried out in order to survey a railroad route to the Pacific. Mountain men, or trappers, are early examples of an American Robinson Crusoe and the early American ideal of masculine values. – William Brandon, *The Men and the Mountain* (William Morrow and Company, 1955), pp. 8f.

Due to the remoteness of his hunting grounds, the Shining Mountains of the Far West, the mountain man was the first inhabitant of America to find himself at ease with the familiar concept of great land distances that Europeans still remark as one of our national attributes. He was seldom a pioneer consciously clearing a way for others to follow – he was only hunting beaver. He was seldom an integrated unit of an organized company, with a big business character branded on his pack, as in the case of the hired pork eaters of the North West Company. He was not a family man in a covered wagon, a settler. He was, at his best, defiantly independent and individual, and he forthrightly referred to himself as free – a free trapper.

He lived on his own in a neolithic world far removed from the Steel Age civilization that had bred him. He brought along only a few of its tools: traps, rifle, knife, awl, powder and lead. He traveled with small, loosely organized groups of his own kind, a handful of men swallowed in an infinity of dark forests and strange winds. His joy was the sensual animal pleasure of life lived for its moments, one by one. He hunted with glowing eyes and spilled blood on pine needles unstirred for centuries.

He owned a mule or horse or two and an Indian girl. He dressed in skins she worked up for him, and she had warm water ready for his feet when he came into his camp from wading the icy beaver streams. In the summer when trading caravans came from St. Louis, he packed the spoils of his year's plunder to the great trappers' rendezvous in the mountains, bartered it for a whoop and a holler and a howling hangover, and set out on the next long hunt.

He floated on the rolling rivers in boats of skin or bark or rafts of logs. He probed out trails that are railroads and highways today, and learned the way from the plains of Kansas to California and from the deserts of New Mexico and Utah to the fern-grown rain forests of Oregon.

Probably the mountain men surpassed the Indians in at least a number of the necessary skills of reading signs, hunting, living off a wild and ominous land, fighting and hiding and running like agile beasts, lying concealed in brush and rocks thoughout a thirsty day if necessary, starving, stealing horses, going dirty, enduring sun and cold and cracking alkali. In some of these things they must have surpassed the Indians to survive, for the Indians were living at home, cushioned by the web of their established society, and the mountain men were interlopers with no support to back them up other than what they carried in their hands, so far in time and space from the established society from which they had sprung that they had all but forgotten its existence.

They were a variegated, highly individualistic bunch, much more so than any vocational group in the confines of civilization. Their lonely, self-sufficient lives developed separatist tendencies, and they were apt at any moment to be subjected to unique experiences for which the group had provided no adjustment, thus inducing bizarre modifications in individuals [...].

They had in common only a constant insecurity and a boundless freedom, both of such dimensions as to be appalling to those sheltered by a civilized world. In their brief time, and it is noteworthy that it was without intention on their part – they were only hunting beaver – the mountain men created a vector of force that was an important factor in extending the sovereignty of the United States over the whole enormous western half of the continent. And coincidentally in their brief time they approached, in a very literal sense, the status of exalted freedom which Rousseau's fantasy portrayed.

Freedom apparently entails challenge and is achieved, not bestowed. The achievement of the mountain men was to go where others had not been, in the face of constant challenge from an awesome and unbroken wilderness. They were repaid in freedom, a freedom they could accept, not being fettered by the fixed taboos and rigid life patterns of their contemporaries, the Indians. They were the freedom fantasy made flesh, even to an uncanny identity with the incidental details of Rousseau's picture: preoccupation with savagery, violence, sensation, and megalomania.

A modern-day mountain man?

Vocabulary

1 remoteness (n.): distance in space or time - **7 beaver** (n.): a water and land animal of the rat family with a broad flat tail and valuable fur - **9 to brand** (v.): to mark s.th. by or as if by burning, esp. to show who owns it - **12 defiant** (adj.): openly and fearlessly refusing to obey, esp. in a way that shows no respect - **13 forthright** (adj.): (too) direct in manner and speech - **18 awl** (n.): a small pointed tool, often with a broad handle, for making holes in leather - **23 to spill** (v.): literary for to cause (blood) to flow by killing or wounding (spilt, spilt, esp. BrE; spilled, spilled, esp. AmE) - **25 mule** (n.): the animal which is the young of a donkey and a usually female horse - **26 to work up** (v.): here to design - **30 spoils** (n.): literary for things taken, esp. by an army from a defeated enemy or by thieves - **30 plunder** (n.): things taken by force and usually violently esp. in time of war or disorder - **31 to barter** (v.): to exchange (goods) for other goods rather than for money - **31 whoop** (n.): /wuːp/ a loud, esp. joyful cry - **32 holler** (n.): esp. AmE for shout - **32 howling** (adj.): very great, extreme - **34 to float** (v.): to stay on the surface of a liquid without - **35 raft** (n.): a flat floating structure, usually made of wood, used as a boat - **35 log** (n.): a thick unshaped piece of wood from a tree - **35 to probe out** (v.): to search or examine - **35 trail** (n): a pass across rough country - **36 plains** (n.): a large stretch of flat land - **37 desert** (n.): /'dezət/ a large sandy piece of land where there is little rain and not much plant life - **38 fern-grown** (adj.): overgrown with a green plant with feathery shaped leaves and no flowers - **39 to surpass** (v.): formal for to go beyond in amount, quality, or degree - **41 ominous** (adj.): giving a warning of s.th. bad that is going to happen - **42 agile** (adj.): /'ædʒaɪl/ able to move quickly and easily - **42f. to conceal** (v.): rather formal for to hide - **43 brush** (n.): here small rough trees and bushes - **47 web** (n.): here network - **49 interloper** (n.): derogatory for a person who enters a place or group with no right to be there - **53 variegated** (adj.): irregular, mixed - **54 vocational** (adj.): professional - **54 confines** (n.): limits or borders - **55 self-sufficient** (adj.): able to provide what one needs without outside help - **56 separatist** (adj.): believing that a particular political or religious group or unit should be separate, and not part of a larger whole - **56 apt** (adj.): likely - **58 adjustment** (n.): slight change, esp. in order to make right or suitable for a purpose or situation - **61 boundless** (adj.): without limits - **62 appalling** (adj.): /ə'pɔːlɪŋ/ shocking, terrible - **69 exalted** (adj.): /ɪg'zɔːltɪd/ literary for filled with a very strong feeling of happiness, power, etc. - **70 fantasy** (n.): s.th. produced from free ima-gination - **71 to entail** (v.): to involve - **71 to achieve** (v.): to get as the result of action or effort - **72 to bestow** (v.): /bɪ'stəʊ/ formal for to give - **76 to fetter** (v.): to prevent from moving as if with chains - **79 uncanny** (adj.): very strange and mysterious - **81 megalomania** (n.): the belief that one is more important, powerful, etc. than one really is

Explanations

1f. the Shining Mountains of the Far West: the Rocky Mountains - **10 North West Company**: a trading company for fur - **15 neolithic**: of the latest period of the Stone Age, about 10,000 years ago, when people began to settle in villages, grow crops, keep animals, polish stone for tools, and use the wheel - **26 skin**: here: the skin of animals for use as leather - **38 rain forest**: a forest with tall trees growing thickly together and with a high rainfall - **45 alkali**: a substance that forms a chemical salt when combined with an acid - **70 Jean Jacques Rousseau**: French philosopher and political theorist (1712-78), who in 1750 chose primitive man, the noble savage dancing in the primeval forest, as his example of individual freedom.

William Brandon (1914 - 2002) was an American free-lance writer of fiction, a historian and a regular contributor to many U.S. magazines. Brandon was born in Kokomo, Indiana, but spent his childhood in several places. His career as a professional writer began in 1938. It was interrupted by his service as a photographer for the United States Army Air Forces in the Pacific Theater during World War II. He is best known for his historical work documenting Native Americans and the American West. His book *The Men and the Mountain*, published in 1955, is an account of John Charles Frémont's failed fourth expedition to the West in 1848 to survey a railroad route to the Pacific Ocean. Frémont was a soldier, explorer, adventurer and later a presidential candidate in the elections of 1856.

Info

Myth

The traditional view of myth is derived from classical Greek "mythos" which signified a story or plot, whether true or invented.
Recently the French structuralist Claude Levi-Strauss has departed from traditional views, in which the definition of myth was very close to that of a legend. He treats the myths of a particular culture as signifying systems whose true meanings are unknown to their proponents. He analyses myths as composed of signs which are to be identified and interpreted on the model of the linguistic theory of Ferdinand de Saussure.
For Levi-Strauss "myth is a structured system of signifiers, whose internal networks of relationships are used to 'map' the structure of other sets of relationships; the 'content' is infinitely variable and relatively unimportant".
This shift of emphasis to myth as a way of thinking with close resemblances to ideology can also be found in the publications of Roland Barthes. Barthes's great achievement was to bring myths home to con-temporary life, to make present-day European readers aware that myths were part of the stuff and fabric of everyday modern life in the West.
If Levi-Strauss sees myth as a kind of thought, for Barthes it is "a type of speech," his emphasis being very similar: "Myth is not defined by the object of its message, but by the way in which it utters its message."
In recent usage then the concepts of myths and ideologies are interlinked: myths perform an ideological function while ideologies function by means of myths.
One should be alert to the bewildering variety of applications of the term "myth" in contemporary literary criticism. Its uses range all the way from signifying any widely held fallacy ("the myth of progress," "the American success myth") to denoting the solidly imagined realm in which a work of fiction is enacted ("the mythical world of *Moby-Dick*").

Background Reading

The mountain men were a mixed bunch, some from good homes, others from the lower strata of society. Some were intelligent, others were mentally defective; there were heroes and victims, villains and clowns. Names to be mentioned in this context are: Jedediah Strong (Jed) Smith, and Kit Carson. Jed Smith was a rather mystical man, the greatest explorer among all the far-ranging mountain men. Kit Carson (1809-1868) is still a dime novel hero. He had been a saddler's apprentice and teamster in the Southwest, but in 1826 became a professional trapper, hunter and guide in the Rocky Mountain Region. He accompanied John C. Frémont on his various journeys of exploration from 1842 to 1847. He had a profound influence on shaping the New West, and he had, according to most contemporary accounts, an exceptional integrity and greatness of soul. He was illiterate (he learned to read during the last few years of his life), modest and taciturn, but accounts of his life have often been glorified to suit fancy rather than fact.

Criticism of the mountain men has also been expressed, e.g. by the British author and traveler Ruxton, who knew the mountain men. "Constantly exposed to perils of all kinds, they become callous to any feeling of danger, and destroy human as well as animal life with as little scruple and as freely as they expose their own. Of laws, human or divine, they neither know nor care to know [...] They may have good qualities, but they are those of the animal. [Some] call them revengeful, blood-thirsty, drunkards, gamblers, regardless of the laws of meum and tuum [...] However, there are exceptions, and I have met honest mountain men." (William Brandon, *The Men and the Mountain.*)

"The American West is Loaded with Myth" Jenni Calder, *There must be a Lone Ranger: The Myth and Reality of the American Wild West* (London: Sphere Books, 1976).

Awareness

1 Write down everything you associate with 'freedom' and compare your notes with your neighbor.
2 As a child, did you enjoy tales like J. Fenimore Cooper's *The Pathfinder* (1840)? Why/Why not?

Comprehension

3 What was the mountain men's main motivation for being in the West?
4 Explain why - according to the author - the mountain men lived in a "neolithic world" (l. 15).
5 On re-reading the text, make at least three statements about what the mountain man was and three about what he was not.
6 What were the mountain man's only social contacts?
7 What does the text say about differences between Native Americans and the mountain men?
8 Even though they are seen as a mixed bunch of people, what – according to the author – do the mountain men have in common?
9 Express in your own words what 'freedom' means in the text.

Analysis

10 Characterize the mountain man's way of life.
11 In how far does the author's choice of words enhance the characterization of the mountain man?
12 What concept of freedom does his way of life reveal? Look at the title of the text, too.

Opinion

13 Discuss whether this concept of freedom could also be realized in an urban area with a high population density.
14 What role do women play in this scenario? Give evidence for your opinion.
15 Complete one of the following sentences: I think the mountain man was a hero because ... . / I do not think that the mountain man was a hero because ... .

Projects

16 With the closing of the frontier in 1890, the era of the mountain men was over. In pairs write your assessment of the future life of the mountain men in society. (How will they earn their living? Will they be able to adapt? Etc.)
17 In groups investigate how the myth of masculinity is reflected in contemporary advertisements (e.g. for cigarettes, spirits, cars, perfume). Make use of the background information on "myth".
18 Watch Baz Luhrmann's film version of Shakespeare's *Romeo and Juliet* and analyse to what effect elements of a Western are used in the showdown between Mercutio and Tybalt (segment 55.04-1.09.21).

Suggested Further Reading

19 Read David Galloway's novel *Tamsen* (New York: Harcourt Brace Jovanovich, 1983), an account of the tragic journey of the Donner party to California in 1846, and find out what dreadful consequences their getting lost in the wilderness was to lead to.

8

Joolz

"Mammy's Boy"

Is maternal feeling based on instinct or conditioning? The cord that unites mother and son may be Western society's most powerful bond, yet attitudes toward the relationship tend to be coated over with clichés. Joolz explores the tension between comedy and tragedy and throws a harsh chilling light on modern life. The following song was written in 1984. - Joolz, *Hex* (Anagram Records, 1990).

He's my son, d'you see, my boy,
my own flesh and blood,
'Cause I love him,
D'you think I give a damn
For your courts of law?
I'd never have given him up, never, never.
He's all I've ever cared about.
Since I carried him,
He's been my world.

Hah, when I was young, they told me
It was all romance, you know,
Well, I saw through that quick enough,
We all do, don't we, lasses?
We have to, by God.
Oh yes, I married his father right enough,
That wasn't hard ... they say
We're the weaker sex ... that's a joke,
I've never known a bloke some girl
Couldn't twist around her little finger
'Aw, don't go to the pub tonight, love,
Don't see those mates of yours,
Why don't you stay here with me
An' have a ... cuddle?
Nine months later it's the altar
An' a home of your own at last.
Oh don't look so shocked
Just because I'll say straight out
What your missus only thinks,
It's the truth, it's the kids we love,
Not you, you pathetic clowns
With your pubs an' beer an' football, hah!
You think you're so tough,
Don't make me laugh ...
You do as much as your woman lets you
An' you never realise.

An' now you're going to take my boy,
My baby, an' you stand there with your
Damned solemn faces an' say,
'But don't you realise, madam,
He has killed three men?'
Well, yes I do, an' what's more I couldn't care less.
He's my child, my child,
An' whatever you do to him,
Wherever you take him
You'll never take him away from me, never.

Mother's Eternal Presence

Joolz was born into an army family in Colchester in 1955, grew up in Portsmouth, and enjoyed reading and writing from a very early age. She spent traumatic teenage years in Harrogate, receiving a private and somewhat unbalanced education. At nineteen, she married a member of a motorcycle gang and moved to Bradford. Incarcerated in gang life for five years, she stopped writing but the knowledge she gained about tribal behaviour became a feature of her later work. After separating from her husband, she eventually turned back to her own writing. Her first book, *Mad, Bad and Dangerous to Know*, was published in 1986, her second collection, *Emotional Terrorism*, in 1990. She has also recorded three albums of poetry (*Never Never Land, Hex* and *Weird Sister*), both solo and with accompanying music, some by New Model Army. Unlike other poets of her generation, Joolz sees poetry not as an entertaining demonstration of irony and wit, nor as an exercise in language and imagery for their own sake. Her principal interest lies in poetry's oldest tradition - that of story-telling, and the examination of character and motivation of ordinary people in extreme situations. In the meantime Joolz has published four novels. Her pen name is Joolz Denby.

Vocabulary

Intro: conditioning (n.): the process by which people or animals are trained to behave in a certain way in certain conditions - **cord** (n.): anything that binds - **chilling** (adj.): causing a cold feeling of fear - **4 I don't give a damn**: informal for I don't care - **13 lass** (n.): (Scottish and Northern English) a girl or young woman - **18 bloke** (n.): informal for a man - **21 mate** (n.): a friend, or person one works with - **23 cuddle** (n.): holding s.o. lovingly and closely in the arms - **28 missus** (n.): informal and old-fashioned for a person's wife - **30 pathetic** (adj.): causing a feeling of pity or sorrow - **38 solemn** (adj.): serious, without humour or lightness

Info

Bonding

The speaker in "Mammy's Boy" frankly admits that she wanted to have a child and does not care about the father very much ("... it's the kids we love, not you, you pathetic clowns", ll. 29f.). In other words her maternal bond is much stronger than that which connects her to the man who has fathered her child. The cartoon on p. 33 satirically highlights the strong bond between a mother and her son.
The Dictionary of Contemporary English defines bonding as a process in which a special relationship develops between two or more people. In the widest possible sense it is the process of establishing human relationships. We differentiate among maternal, paternal, friendship and other forms of bonding. The maternal bond describes the relationship between a mother and her child. It begins during pregnancy and can be enhanced - according to recent research - by sonograms of the fetus. The process of bonding is hardly ever instantaneous - as most people falsely think - but will develop within hours, days or weeks. Moreover, it is influenced by a variety of emotional, physical and social factors.
Ideally, the maternal bond is supplemented by the paternal bond. Attachment to the unborn child will develop during the partner's pregnancy. Research has shown that a few months before birth male testosterone levels sink, making men more caring and softer and thus preparing them for the new paternal bond. Bonding can also be achieved when fathers bathe soothe, feed, carry or soothe the baby. In the early stages of a child's development child-parent interaction develops in different ways, which gradually leads to an attachment bond formed between them.
In popular gender studies the terms male and female bonding are widely used, sometimes humorously, to describe the activity of doing things with members of the same sex so that you feel good about being a man or a woman. Whereas men prefer to be bonded by shared activities, women predominantly use emotional sharing.

Awareness

1 Even mass murderers, terrorists or religious fanatics have parents. Imagine you are the father/mother of such a person, what would be your parental feelings?
2 Imagine you were a parent. Outline your idea of the parental role.

Comprehension

3 Who are the men with their "damned solemn faces" (l. 38)?
4 Who is the speaker?

Analysis

5 Where does the conversation take place?
6 Describe the speaker's view of men and of women by referring to the examples of their behaviour mentioned in the text.
7 Characterize the general tone of what the speaker says. How is it achieved?
8 The song breaks into three stanzas. Analyse their structure, concentrating on the speaker's train of thought.

Opinion

9 How old do you think the son is?
10 Working in pairs, make up a story about what happened: in what circumstances did the triple murder take place?
11 Do you think that a strong mother-son relationship is beneficial or detrimental to the psychological well-being of the child? Give reasons for your opinion.

Projects

12 Put yourself in the role of a court psychiatrist and try to characterise the relationship between mother and son. Draw up a written report to be submitted to the court.
13 Write a letter to Joolz describing your reactions to and (mixed?) feelings about the song.
Joolz
P.O. Box 162
Bradford BD3 8YH, West Yorkshire, UK

Internet Project

14 Check the Internet for background information on 'Momism' and 'New Momism'. www.usatoday.com, www.cbsnews.com/stories and www.princeton.edu/rbsc/fellowships might help you in your research.

Suggested Further Reading

15 Read Susan Douglas' and Meredith Michaels' book *The Mommy Myth* (New York: Simon and Schuster, 2004).

Info

Momism

Momism goes back to the 1940s, when American author Philip Wylie (1902-1971) coined the phrase. In his bestseller *Generation of Vipers*, "a satiric critique of American morals and manners" (published in 1942), he was opposed to the "iconic all-American mother" and declared that the nation were affected by 'momism'. This term was adopted by psychologists and sociologists to describe the social role of a mother who lives 'through' her children or bases her entire existence exclusively on motherhood. One of Wylie's aims was to alert women to the possibly pathological consequences of stifling mother love - both for the mother and the child. Experts who followed Wylie's ideas did not deny the importance of early mother-child-bonding, but at the same time rejected crippling generational dependency and propagated a more influential role of fathers. Wylie's book thus became seminal and helped "to reshape mainstream gender ideology in the mid-twentieth century U.S.".
At the turn of the 21st century we are confronted with the concept of the "new Momism". In an interview Susan Douglas, co-author of *The Mommy Myth* (New York, 2004), defines it as "a highly romanticized myth of the perfect mother". She claims that "it's a role no woman can ever attain. Her 'to do' list includes piping Mozart into her womb, using algebra flash cards with her 6-month-old, teaching her 3-year-old to read James Joyce, driving five hours to a soccer match, and oh, yes, being sexy and cheerful through all of this." In her analysis she diagnoses four aspects that have created the new Mom: "Fear, fantasy, marketing and politics." Her political credo is that "motherhood is the unfinished business of the women's movement."(www.princeton.edu/rbsc/fellowships/2003-04; www.cbsnews.com/stories/2004/02/05/earlyshow/leisure/books)

9

Peter Redgrove

"Early Morning Feed"

The following poem was published in an anthology entitled *The New Poetry*, which is a collection of poetry written in the 1960s. Here Redgrove, a Cambridge graduate born in 1932, presents his attitude towards his baby son. – Peter Redgrove, "Early Morning Feed", *The New Poetry*, ed. by A. Alvarez (Harmondsworth: Penguin, repr. 1966), pp. 215f.

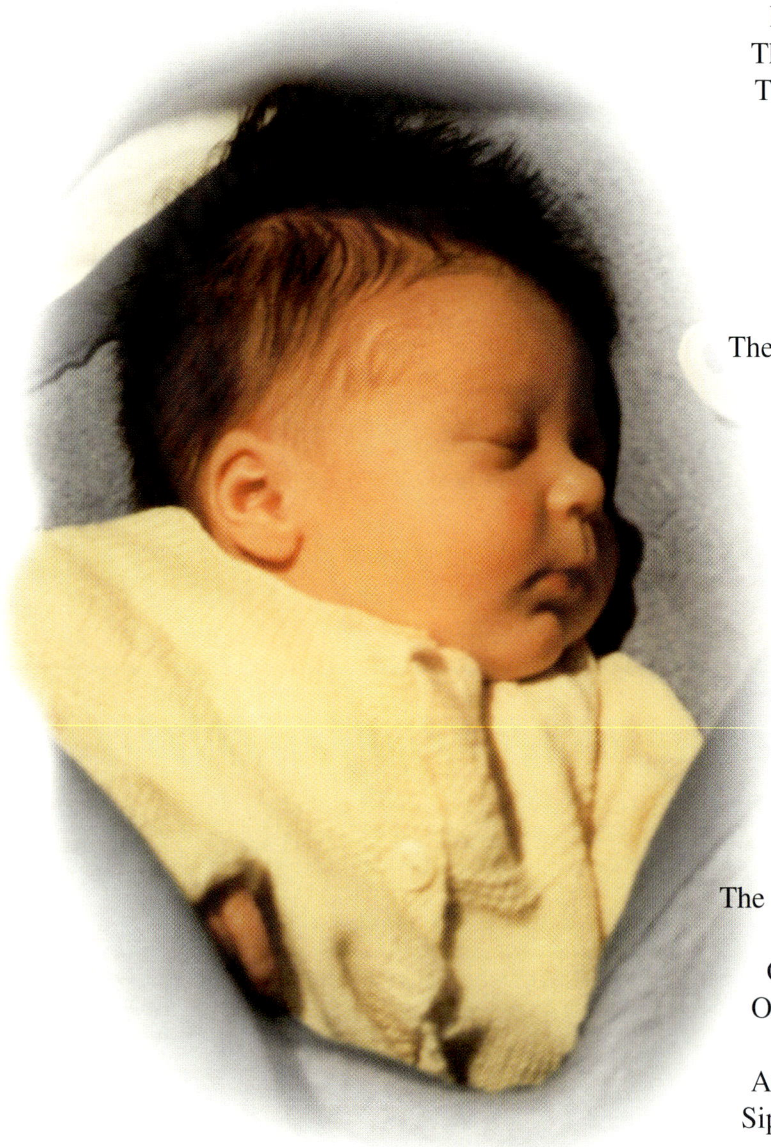

The father darts out on the stairs
To listen to that keening
In the upper room, for a change of note
That signifies distress, to scotch disaster,
The kettle humming in the room behind.

He thinks, on tiptoe, ears a-strain,
The cool dawn rising like the moon:
'Must not appear and pick him up;
He mustn't think he has me springing
To his beck and call',
The kettle rattling behind the kitchen door.

He has him springing
A-quiver on the landing –
For a distress-note, a change of key,
To gallop up the stairs to him
To take him up, light as a violin,
And stroke his back until he smiles.
He sidles in the kitchen
And pours his tea ...

And again stands hearkening
For milk cracking the lungs.
There's a little panting,
A cough: the thumb's in: he'll sleep,
The cup of tea cooling on the kitchen table.

Can he go in now to his chair and think
Of the miracle of breath, pick up a book,
Ready at all times to take it at a run
And intervene between him and disaster,
Sipping his cold tea as the sun comes up?

He returns to bed
And feels like something, with the door ajar,
Crouched in the bracken, alert, with big eyes
For the hunter, death, disaster.

Peter (William) Redgrove was born in Kingston, Surrey, in 1932, educated at Taunton School, and graduated from King's College, Cambridge. He has four children from two marriages. He has held various professorships and lectured abroad. He received several Arts Council grants and won the Guardian Prize for Fiction in 1973. Redgrove now lives in Falmouth, Cornwall. In addition to his verse, for which he is known best, he has also published plays and novels. Peter Redgrove wrote in *The Guardian*, 12 April 1979: "The most ordinary people have the most extraordinary dreams, and in them have a capacity for understanding and adaptation far beyond their waking lives. Why do we so taboo the dream life when it is so plainly a continuum with the waking creative imagination?"

Vocabulary

1 to dart (v.): to move suddenly and quickly - **2 keening** (n.): utterance in a wailing tone - **4 distress** (n.): pain or great discomfort - **4 to scotch** (v.): formal for to put an end to - **5 to hum** (v.): to make a continuous low sound - **6 on tiptoe** (n.): on one's toes with the rest of the feet raised above the ground - **6 a-strain**: in a state of worried concentration - **7 dawn** (n.): the time of day, when light first appears - **9 to spring** (v.): to appear or come into action quickly or from nothing - **10 at s.o.'s beck and call**: always ready to do anything s.o. asks - **13 aquiver**: in a slight trembling movement, esp. from fear or excitement - **13 landing** (n.): the level space at the top of a set of stairs or between two sets of stairs - **18 to sidle** (v.): to move uncertainly or secretly - **20 to hearken** (v.): literary for to listen - **21 to crack** (v.): to split - **22 panting** (n.): quick, short breaths - **28 to intervene** (v.): to interrupt, esp. in order to prevent a bad result - **31 ajar** (adj., adv.): /əˈdʒɑː/ not quite closed, slightly open - **32 to crouch** (v.): to lower the body closer to the ground by bending the knees - **32 bracken** (n.): a plant (a kind of fern) which commonly grows in woods and forests, etc., and becomes a rich red-brown in autumn - **32 alert** (adj.): watchful and ready to deal with danger

Awareness

1 One of the unsolved medical problems of today is the Sudden Infant Death Syndrome, in Britain colloquially called 'cot death'. Try to describe the feelings of parents who find that their healthy baby has died unexpectedly and inexplicably.

Comprehension

2 Explain the title of the poem.
3 What is the approximate age of the son?
4 What is the father listening to?
5 What is the role of the father?
6 Explain the simile the author uses in the last stanza.

Analysis

7 Fear and panic are the overall feelings evoked in the poem. How are they created?
8 Analyse the structure of the poem and determine what it contributes to the effect the poem has on the reader.
9 Compare the father-son relationship in this poem with the mother-son relationship in "Mammy's Boy".

Opinion

10 Discuss the obvious contradiction between the statement "He mustn't think he has me springing to his beck and call" (ll. 9f.) and the father's actual reactions.
11 Where do you think the mother is? Why is she not mentioned?
12 Do you think the father is overprotective? Give reasons for your opinion.
13 In the U.S., and also in Britain, groups like the National Coalition of Free Men, Men's Rights Inc. or fathers' rights organisations have been established. What could be the motivations of the men's rights activists who join them?

Project

14 Write a bedtime story for the son in the poem.
15 Find out about child/parent bonding by checking an encyclopedia of psychology. Are there any differences between male and female ways of bonding?

Internet Project

16 Go to www.dadsmagazine.com and get information about different father-child relationships and the emotional attachments involved.

10

"The myth of Super Dad"

From the new man of the 1980s via the smug dad to the super dad: how are male roles to be defined? Is this reality or simply a media hype? New Labour suddenly wants to be seen as the party of new fatherhood. It should take a reality check, says Dylan Jones, editor of GQ magazine and author of the following article. - *The Sunday Times,* 13 April 2003.

Tony Blair: Master of the Universe, New Man, Smug Dad, Super Dad – or just a dad who loves his children?

Last week saw the publication of two magazine interviews with the prime minister, both of which focused on his ability to juggle invading politically unstable Middle Eastern fiefdoms while looking at a rumbustious three-year-old. As Blair turns 50 he obviously feels the need to impress upon us the fact that he is a family man at heart.

In an interview with *She magazine,* Blair, posing for the pictures with Cherie in a crisp white shirt, offered some tantalising insights into his working day.

"You know what children are like," he said. "Kathryn's having a problem with her homework or Leo wants to play. One of the advantages of living above 'the shop' is that it's easy to pop up during the day. Or Leo comes down. I've got a fruit bowl in my office and he brings me fruit in a little trolley."

Apart from being a tremendous scoop on behalf of *She,* the magazine "for women who juggle their lives", this showed Blair trying to woo back waning female support for Labour.

A few days later, he was doing it again, this time in *Saga* magazine, which is aimed at older women. "Upstairs in Blair's office, I asked the prime minister if Leo keeps him young,"writes the interviewer, Valerie Grove. "He certainly does," replies Blair, "especially when he wakes us up in the night, as he does rather frequently."

Who gets up to him? "Well, with our first three kids that was always my job. I'm afraid, especially recently, I have left it to Cherie."[...]

And then, to compound this onslaught of domesticity, 250,000 copies of a new trade department-funded magazine hits the newsstands and maternity wards: *Dad,* "the magazine for new fathers", designed to spread the word about recent paternity leave legislation and to make new dads better informed and more confident about their rights and responsibilities.

[...]

"Fathers have been left out of the family debate too long. There is a huge programme of support for mothers and rightly so,"[Patricia Hewitt, the secretary for trade and industry] told The Sunday Times. "When you get pregnant there are antenatal classes, support networks, and then, when you actually have the baby as well as the direct support you're getting from the health service there's also a huge amount of information and advice, a bagful of products that you are given while you are still in the maternity ward. For men, for the fathers, there is almost nothing."

So why all this interest in modern fatherhood ? Are we witnessing the return of the New Man? One can never put the appearance of interviews with the prime minister down to happenstance. Even if the readers of *She* and *Saga* have not been the victims of spin, one can't deny that Labour has brought the topic of fatherhood close to the top of its domestic agenda.

When it swept into power in 1997, the concept of the new dad seemed to be one of the (many) defining characteristics of the government's lifestyle manifesto. New Labour espoused modernity, egalitarianism and inclusivity, and a free tall skinny latte with every order.

Part of the manifesto determined that if you were a man it was okay to be the master of the universe as long as you spent serious quality time with the kids when you got home. But in terms of legislation, government policy focused far more on the rights of mothers (maternity leave, flexibility for working mums).

From this month, however, fathers have the right to two weeks' paid paternity leave – as long as they give three months' notice – and nearly 400,000 fathers each year are expected to take up this offer. Plus, fathers of young disabled children will get the right, like mothers, to work flexible hours.

"There are more and more surveys showing that fathers want to play a more active part in their children's lives than their own fathers did with them,"Hewitt says. This may be true, but how many of them are able to? Even if they have the inclination, few British men have the time to play superdad.

British men work the longest hours in Europe; fewer than 15% of fathers with young children have flexible working hours; only 3% of all male workers have a jobshare; around one in eight working fathers work 60 or more hours a week, and over a third work more then 48 hours. Then there are the men who do not even have free access to their children: divorce rates have never been higher.

In many ways Labour is behind the curve in trying to encourage men to be a little more touchy-feely.

If one thinks back to the early 1990s, to a time when "yuppie"was officially a pejorative and when the all-new male consumer was beginning to tire of his mattblack designer home, and when advertisers were trying to find new ways in which to ensnare him, the New Man was born.

The new man, in case you have forgotten, was the caring-sharing type, the sort of guy who dressed in fancy designer clothes, who drove a souped-up Gti and who frequented fashionable riverside cocktail bars; but he was also the kind of guy who got up in the middle of the night to comfort his newborn baby, who wasn't afraid to push a pram through the park (Afraid! Ha! He loved it, looked forward to it!), who was quite willing to while away the hours discussing his feelings with his girlfriend's girlfriends as they all knocked back the Aqua Libra.

The advertising of this period reflects the new man, too: Armani, Gillette, Calvin Klein, Quorum and Next commissioned ads featuring well-groomed, well-dressed thirtysomething men with uncharacteristically serene babies.

Ah, this was the new "kinder, gentler", politically correct lifestyle made manifest. Glossy magazines soon followed suit, and these ads appeared opposite pages and pages devoted to media-savvy gadabouts pictured hugging offspring who seemed strangely intrigued to see their parents so close-up.

But the new man was an adland fantasy. Even the original new man poster boy, Mark Perry, turned out to be something of an unreconstructed lad. Perry, you may remember, was the male model who became famous as a pin-up of the early 1980s.

Looking not unlike James Dean, and stripped to the waist, Perry appeared in an astonishingly popular poster posing with a newborn baby.

The photograph was shot, oh-so tastefully, in black and white and became as popular as posters of Garfield or Adam Ant on female dormitory walls from St. Paul's to St. Mary's, Calne.

But Perry later wrote a book in which he claimed to have slept with more than 3,000 women between the ages of 15 and 33. Whether he was a lothario or a fantasist, he was hardly a new man. None of us was. He was a media creation, one which even the most cynical of us couldn't bring ourselves to buy into.

The prime minister himself isn't so much new man as Smug Dad, and while it would be unfair to say that Blair has exploited his family unit it won't have escaped anyone's notice that his family has helped enormously with his public image.

Smug Dads are those fathers who are overtly affectionate and extravagantly show-offy about their children. "Smug Dad syndrome manifests itself in many ways, but the early telltale signs are fairly easy to spot,"says one male friend of mine, a father of two who is himself something of a designer dad.

"Tick more than two of any of the following boxes and you can diagnose yourself with SDS, too. Do you insist on feeding/holding/changing your baby's nappies in public/or at parties even though you might never go near it at home?"

"Do you play loud, ostentatious rough and tumble games in the park in close proximity to childless couples? Are you the owner of a nonsensical pavement-hogging off-road baby buggy imported from America via the web, which was bought simply for the reason that Tom Cruise has one?"

Smug Dads are everywhere."I can't believe how tiredness has become such a furiously competitive game of one-upmanship with all the dads I know,"said television presenter Johnny Vaughan last week.

"I was in a meeting the other morning and a dad I work with rolled in looking shattered. The conversation went something like this:'How long did you get last night?' 'An hour and a half at most.' 'Really? Ours just sleeps for 20 minutes at a time at the moment. It's a nightmare.' Then, from the other side of the table another dad's voice piped up, 'Just the one is it? You wait until you've got two. That's when the real nightmares start'."

I must admit I was something of a smug dad when my first daughter was born, and I proudly stalked aound the office banging on about how little sleep I had had, how one of my arms was becoming longer than the other due to excessive midnight cradle rocking.

But soon I realized how facile this was. I wasn't really doing the work, I was just talking about it. I wasn't up all hours breastfeeding, I was trying to take the glory. I was just, after all, a typical man, not a new man at all, not even a new lad. And certainly not a superdad.

Justine Roberts, the founder of mumsnet.com, Britain's most popular parenting website where mothers swap advice on men and childcare, says superdads are few and far between.

"He's still definitely the exception and not the rule. We've recently conducted a survey on the state of modern motherhood and women are still doing the bulk of the childcaring. I wouldn't poohpooh these government initiatives ... but I don't know how much men are really interested. I think a lot of men still think of raising children as women's work."

Superdads are, like new men, simply mythical creatures. If one were a cynical person, one could imagine the conceit of the new government legislation and interest in fatherhood as simply a ploy to appeal, not to modern men, but to women voters. [...]

"I'M JUST WORKING OUT THE BEST TIME TO TAKE PATERNITY LEAVE."

Vocabulary

6 to juggle (v.): to try to fit two or more jobs, activities etc. into your life - **8 fiefdom** (n.): a feudal organisation - **9 rumbustious** (adj.): full of energy, fun and noise - **19 tantalising** (adj.): making you feel a strong desire to have or do s.th. - **31 scoop** (n.): an important or exciting news story that is printed in one newspaper before any of the others know about it - **33 to woo** (v.): to try and persuade s.o. to do s.th. such as buy s.th from you, vote for you, or work for you - **33 waning** (adj.): becoming gradually less strong or less important - **44 to compound** (v.): to make a difficult situation worse by adding more problems - **44 onslaught** (n.): /ɒnslɔːt/ the effect of s.th. that is unpleasant and could cause damage - **44 domesticity** (n.): life at home with your family - **47 maternity** (adj.): relating to a woman who is pregnant or who has just had a baby - **48 ward** (n.): a large room in a hospital where people who need medical treatment stay - **51 paternity leave** (n.): a period of time that the father of a new baby is allowed to stay away from work - **52 legislation** (n.): a law or a set of laws - **67 antenatal** (adj.): (BrE) /æntɪneɪtl/ relating to the medical care given to women who are going to have a baby - **80 happenstance** (n.): chance, or s.th. that happens by chance - **81 spin** (n.): the way s.o., especially a politician or business person, talks about information or a situation, especially in order to influence the way people think about it - **86 manifesto** (n.): a written statement by a political party, saying what they believe in and what they intend to do - **87 to espouse** (v.): (formal) /ɪ'spaʊz/ to support an idea, belief etc, especially a political one - **87 egalitarianism** (n.): belief that everyone is equal and should have equal rights - **91 quality time** (n.): the time that you spend giving s.o. your full attention, especially time you spend with your children when you are not busy - **105 inclination** (n.): a feeling that makes you want to do s.th. - **116 touchy-feely**

(adj.): too concerned with feelings and emotions, rather than with facts or actions - **118 pejorative** (adj.): (formal) used to show disapproval or to insult s.o. - **121 to ensnare** (v.): (formal) to trap s.o. in an unpleasant or illegal situation, from which they cannot escape - **125 souped-up** (adj.): used for a car that has been made more powerful - **130f. to while away the hours**: to spend time in a pleasant and lazy way - **136 serene** (adj.): very calm or peaceful - **141 media-savvy** (adj.): s.o. who knows how to deal with the media - **141 gadabout** (n.): (informal) s.o. who goes out a lot or travels a lot in order to enjoy themselves - **144 adland** (n.): the activity or business of advertising, considered as a whole - **194 to pipe up** (v.): (informal) to suddenly say s.th. especially when you have been quiet until then - **217 mythical** (adj.): imagined or invented - **218 cynical** (adj.): unwilling to believe that people have good, honest, or sincere reasons for doing s.th. - **219 conceit** (n.): an attitude that shows you have too high an opinion of your own abilities or importance - **220 ploy** (n.): a clever and dishonest way of tricking s.o. so that you can get an advantage

Explanations

Title: myth: see info box on p. 31 - **Intro: GQ**: a magazine for men including news on lifestyle and fashion - **45 trade department-funded**: the money has been provided by the department of trade and industry; the secretary of state for trade and industry was Patricia Hewitt (later secretary of state for the health service) - **78 New Man**: a man who is considered to be very modern because he shares the work of looking after his children, cooking, cleaning the home etc. - **132 Aqua Libra**: trademark for a refreshing drink made with fruit juices and natural herbal extracts - **134 Armani, Gillette, Calvin Klein, Quorum, Next**: are all trademarks for various products which men associate with - **153 Garfield**: a cartoon cat - **154 Adam Ant**: lead singer of the pop group Adam and the Ants, famous in the early 1980s, before he started a solo career - **154 St. Paul's**: an independent boys' school in London - **155 St. Mary's, Calne**: an independent girls' school - **158 lothario** (n.): (lit.or derog.) a man whose main interest is having as many female lovers as possible without having a serious relationship with any of them

Awareness

1 Try and remember who looked after you when you were a baby, a toddler or an infant.
2 Were there any differences in the nurture / care you got from your father or your mother?
3 Did your father change your nappies?

Comprehension

4 How does Tony Blair talk about his children and why does it surprise the reader?
5 What is meant by the Smug Dad Syndrome (SDS) (ll. 169f.) and how can one "diagnose"it?
6 What, according to the author, is the role of the media in the creation of the image of the Super Dad?
7 Explain why Mark Perry obviously did not qualify as the New Man.

Analysis

8 Characterise the following male figures:
- the Super Dad
- the New Man
- the Smug Dad.

9 Analyse the author's presentation of the topic and find out whose side he is on.
10 Outline the public image of Tony Blair that is evoked in this article.

Project

11 Imagine you are a hard-working father of a toddler or of a teenager. How would you spend "quality time" with them? Work together in groups and design a schedule.
12 Play the role of a public relations expert who has to design the public image of celebrities. Design the public images of a male and a female celebrity, e.g. David Beckham and Leila Ali.

Internet Project

13 Check http://www.mumsnet.com, "Britain's most popular parenting website" (ll. 206f.) and find out what topics are dealt with. Why do you think it is called "mumsnet", if it deals with parenting?
14 If you want to know, e.g. how the New Man dresses for a summer's evening, go to http://men.style.com.

Further Reading

15 R. E. Page, "Cherie: Lawyer, Wife, Mum: Contradictory Patterns of Representation in Media Reports of Cherie Booth/Blair", *Discourse Society,* Sept. 1, 2003; 14(5); pp. 559-579.

11

Fun Quiz: Are you hetero, metro or completely off the dial?

According to Mark Bowness, author of the following text, "Britain is in the grip of a cross-dressing fervour, with blokes turning into skirt-wearing, air-kissing, lipstick-chomping she-males". " [The] new buzzword for men who care for their appearance, take an interest in designer labels, enjoy cooking and are not afraid to show their feminine side is 'metrosexual'. Celebs have long been into cross-dressing. David Beckham with his sarong, love for Posh's knickers and nail varnish has been joined by Robbie Williams (and others) who have all stepped out in skirts." If you want to find out, if Britain is "really met or het and where you really stand" in this, complete the following quiz and all will be revealed. - *The Sun*, December 11, 2003.

1. You think exfoliation is:

a) Napalming jungle areas in combat zones.
b) For cissies.
c) Removing dead skin cells.
d) Essential once a week.

2. You need a haircut. Do you go to:

a) The kitchen for a pudding bowl and scissors?
b) A barber?
c) A hairdresser?
d) A salon?

3. The proper greeting for a male friend is:

a) A grunt.
b) A firm handshake and a manly hug.
c) A kiss on both cheeks.
d) Running at each other from five feet apart, yelling: "Dah-ling!"

4. The dominant colour in your wardrobe is:

a) Black.
b) Blue.
c) Deep plum - it's all the rage at Paul Smith!
d) Cerise.

5. Which beauty products do you use?

a) Toothpaste.
b) Aftershave, on special occasions.
c) Moisturiser and hair gel.
d) Cleanser, toner, moisturiser, foundation, exfoliator, face pack ...

6. Lunchtime consists of:

a) Two pints of strong lager and a packet of pork scratchings.
b) Nothing. Lunch is for wimps.
c) Sushi.
d) A lightly-tossed green salad and a glass of pink champagne.

7. Your best mate invites you for a night out. Do you suggest:

a) Starting early on a pub crawl, then heading for the local strip club?
b) A game of darts in the local?
c) Late-night shopping before watching the match over gin and tonics in a trendy sports bar?
d) A trip to see the movie Love Actually?

8. You are given free tickets to see the next England rugby game. Your first reaction is:

a) Brilliant - a ten-hour drinking session.
b) Can't wait to see the game.
c) Who else is going to be there?
d) Can't wait to see Jonny Wilkinson's legs.

9. The office Christmas party is fancy dress. What do you go as:

a) John Wayne?
b) David Brent?
c) David Bowie?
d) Judy Garland?

10. **Your favourite coffee table magazine is:**

a) Big and Bouncy
b) Loaded
c) Men's Health
d) Cosmopolitan

11. **Your partner suggests you go Christmas shopping together. Your reaction is:**

a) Don't be so bloody stupid.
b) I'll miss the match.
c) OK, meet you in Top Shop.
d) Only if he promises not to throw a hissy fit this year.

12. **Out shopping you are always finding yourself:**

a) Drifting towards the pub.
b) Drifting in and out of consciousness.
c) Drifting in and out of French Connection.
d) Drifting in and out of the changing room trying on about 50 different outfits.

13. **Your record collection includes:**

a) Iron Maiden and Limp Bizkit.
b) The Darkness.
c) Dido.
d) Gloria Gaynor.

14. **You are asked to take part in your child's school sports day. What event do you choose to compete in:**

a) 100m sprint?
b) Egg and spoon race?
c) Nothing - you can't run in a skirt.
d) I don't do sports, darlin'.

15. **You are best man at your Scottish friend's wedding. At the fitting you tell the groom:**

a) I'll wear whatever you want me to, apart from a stupid bloody skirt.
b) I'll wear the kilt if I really have to.
c) I'm not wearing a kilt unless it's the right label.
d) Does my bum look big in this little number?

How would he rate: A, B, C, D?

16. **You win backstage tickets to meet Shirley Bassey after her concert. What do you do:**

a) Flog them on eBay?
b) Agree to take your mother?
c) You'd love to go but it clashes with the opening of that trendy bar up West?
d) Wet yourself?

17. **What do you think of cross-dressing Eddie Izzard :**

a) You despise the ground he totters about on.
b) Live and let live.
c) You love his new outfit.
d) You adore him, but someone should tell him that's the wrong shade of lippy for that dress.

18. **It's your grandparent' 60th wedding anniversary. What do you wear:**

a) A football scarf - you're going to the match instead?
b) A smart and sensible suit?
c) A silk shirt?
d) A pair of your wife's knickers and a push-up bra?

19. **What is your favourite TV programme:**

a) The Premiership?
b) The Office?
c) Sex and the City?
d) Acorn Antiques?

20. **What is the first thing you pack when you go on holiday:**

a) Knotted hankie?
b) A packet of condoms?
c) Factor 25 sun cream with extra protection for dry skin?
d) Sequinned beach shorts?

21. **A fire breaks out in your house and you only have time to take one thing - what do you grab:**

a) Your Debbie Does Dallas video?
b) Your dog?
c) Your favourite sarong?
d) Your original Chicago soundtrack?

22. **A bloke comes up to you in the pub and mistakes you for a lady. What do you do?**

a) Smack him in the face?
b) Tell him he's got the wrong person?
c) Tell him where you got your outfit?
d) Grab your coat and tell him he's pulled?

23. **You wake up in the morning and your first thought is:**

a) I wonder if the missus fancies a quickie.
b) What a great game on TV last night. I can't wait to read the match reports.
c) My skin feels dry. I need to moisturise.
d) God! I've only got two hours to soak in the bath, do my hair, paint my nails and decide what to wear.

24. **The first thing you do when you get in the office is:**

a) Have a canteen fry-up and head to trap two with your morning paper.
a) Discuss the latest soccer results and last night's TV.
a) Make coffee for everyone and discuss the new fine art exhibition.
a) Head to the toilets and touch up your make-up before having a gossip about who pulled who the night before.

Be honest, guys, how did you rate?

Mostly As:
You've got nothing to worry about and you are a 100 per cent macho male.

Mostly Bs:
You're all male but you've got an open mind.

Mostly Cs:
Eat your heart out, David Beckham. You're a fully signed-up metrosexual.

Mostly Ds:
You're so in touch with your feminine side you'll be needing evening primrose oil soon.

Vocabulary

Title: to be off the dial: (informal) to be incalculable - **Intro: cross-dressing** (adj.): wearing clothes usually worn by a person of the opposite sex - **fervour** (n.): very strong feelings about s.th. - **air-kissing** (adj.): greeting s.o. with a kiss that is near the side of their face, but that does not touch them - **lipstick-chomping** (adj.): lipstick-eating - **celeb** (n.): (informal) celebrity - **1 exfoliation** (n.): removal of dead cells from your skin to make it smoother - **3 cissy** (n.): (=sissy) (informal, impolite) a boy that other boys dislike because he prefers doing things that girls enjoy - **9 barber** (n.): a man whose job is to cut men's hair and sometimes to shave them - **13 grunt** (n.): a short low sound that a person or animal makes in their throat - **23 cerise** (n.): /səri:s/ a bright pinkish-red colour - **33 wimp** (n.): (informal) s.o. who has a weak character and is afraid to do s.th. difficult or unpleasant - **69 hissy fit** (n.): (informal) a sudden moment of unreasonable anger and annoyance - **103 to flog** (v.): (informal) to sell - **110 to totter** (v.): to walk or move unsteadily from side to side as if you are going to fall - **115 lippy** (n.): (BrE, informal) lipstick - **132 knotted** (adj.): tied in a knot or in several knots - **136 sequinned** (adj.): /si:kwɪnd/ decorated with small shiny flat pieces of metal, sewn onto clothes - **150 to pull** (v.): (BrE, spoken) to attract s.o. in order to have sex with them or spend the evening with them - **162 fry-up** (BrE, informal) a meal of fried food such as eggs, bacon, potatoes etc.

"I know real men cry these days, Gerald, but not for getting soap in their eyes."

Explanations

Intro/5 sarong (n.): a loose skirt consisting of a long piece of cloth wrapped around your waist, worn especially by people in Malaysia and Indonesia - **2 napalm** (n.): a substance made from petrol that was used in bombs by US forces to burn fields and villages in the Vietnam war - **22 Paul Smith**: a famous fashion designer, originally from Nottingham, with outlets all over the world - **32 pork scratchings** (n.): small pieces of pig's skin that have been cooked in hot fat and are eaten cold - **45 *Love Actually***: movie (featuring Bill Nighy) about several people who do not have much in common, but come together eventually; in this movie love is the most important raison d'être - **52 Jonny Wilkinson**: fly-half on English rugby team - **55 John Wayne (1907-79)**: an American film actor, who played honest, strong, independent and patriotic characters; he was thought to be an example of a good American - **56 David Brent**: was the regional manager of an office in Slough and appeared in the BBC documentary comedy The Office - **57 David Bowie**: an English songwriter and singer of popular music, who has also acted in plays and films - **58 Judy Garland**: (1922-69) an American film actress and singer who was most famous as the character of Dorothy in the film *The Wizard of Oz* - **60 *Big And Bouncy***: a men's magazine - **61 *Loaded***: another men's magazine, first published 1994, which covered the lad culture of the 1990s like no other and glorified British male "rogues"- **63 *Cosmopolitan***: a monthly magazine for women produced in both Britain and the US in different versions. In Britain it has an image which is intended to attract the more modern, young, independent and cosmopolitan reader. In the US it is very often critizised by feminists for being old-fashioned in its views of men and women. - **68 Top Shop**: tdmk., fashion store with outlets all over Britain - **75 French Connection**: tdmk., a London-based fashion company with international outlets - **79 Iron Maiden**: a British heavy-metal band which was founded in the 1980s - **79 Limp Bizkit**: a hard rock/hip-hop fusion band, formed 1994 in Jacksonville, Florida - **80 The Darkness**: successful British hard-rock band, founded in 2002 - **81 Dido**: British female pop singer from north London, successful since 1999 - **82 Gloria Gaynor**: an American disco singer, born 1949 in Newark, New Jersey; two of her titles, "I will survive" and "I am what I am", figure as unofficial hymns for homosexuals - **101 Shirley Bassey**: a British popular music singer, born in Cardiff in 1937, known for her sexually attractive appearance and exciting stage performances, e.g. in Las Vegas - **109 Eddie Izzard**: British actor and stand-up comedian, born 1962 in Jemen, who likes to appear as a transvestite - **126 The Premiership**: soccer programme on BBCSport - **127 *The Office***: British docu-com from the BBC about office life - **129** ***Acorn Antiques***: British soap - **140** ***Debbie Does Dallas***: a pornographic film, published in 1978, considered to be a classic in its genre - **143** ***Chicago***: musical film featuring Richard Gere and Catherine Zeta-Jones - **175** **evening primrose oil**: used as a treatment for a number of diseases, esp. those related to menstruation and the menopause

Awareness

1 a) When you are waiting at the dentist's or the hairdresser's, do you ever feel tempted to do the 'psychological' tests in the magazines provided?
b) Can you explain the motivation behind the 'compulsion' that many people feel?

Analysis

2 Explain the humour in the headline of the quiz.
3 Define the concepts of masculinity employed in this test.
4 Check the four categories of answers and write character sketches for the four clichés of men.
5 Analyse the linguistic style in which this test is written. Bear in mind that *The Sun* belongs to the yellow press.

Project

6 "A day in the life of ... " Write four diary entries, one for each of the four male stereotypes.
7 Find advertisements from a magazine or newspaper and analyse how myths of femininity/masculinity are employed.

Internet Project

8 Use the Internet to collect information about concepts of femininity and masculinity. www.wikipedia.de might be a good starting point.

12 "The new ladette or: Call my bluff?"*

Girls know how to have fun. Forget about sugar and spice! It's o.k. to be "a bit of a lad"! Or is it? Women are swilling lager and wolf-whistling with the best of them. David Thomas, the author of this article, happily relinquishes the male monopoly on blokish behaviour. - *The Sunday Times,* 19 February 1995.

Well, you can forget about that sugar-and-spice stuff, for a start. These days, girls are made of sterner stuff. A recent survey carried out by the AA showed that 54% of women questioned admitted acts of aggression on the road. The number of women jailed for motoring-related crimes has doubled in the past year. [...]

In general, women still commit far fewer crimes than men, but the rate at which their offences are increasing is much greater, so the gap is gradually narrowing. What makes young women act in this way? Well, one important factor in male crime is alcohol abuse, and here, too, the sexes are well on the road to equality.

The Brewer's & Licensed Retailers Association predicts that by the year 2000 half of all pub-goers will be women. And they won't be sipping Babychams, either. Women make up one-third of all lager drinkers and one-sixth of ale buffs, according to a survey by the brewers Carlsberg-Tetley. There is an increasing number of all-girl drinking clubs, too. Especially on university campuses, such as Cambridge, for example. [...]

When the advertising agency Collett Dickenson Pearce compiled a marketing study called *A Portrait of Lads,* it found that 550,000 of the 2m young adults who fitted the criteria of being single, drinking more than eight pints a week, and having laddish attitudes, were female. So, is there a new generation of ladettes, or faux-blokes?

Sometimes it seems that way, as a slew of jeans and cola ads feature gangs of girls leering at cute young hunks or leaning out of windows to wolf-whistle beefy builders. At last year's Miss UK beauty competition, a Mr UK contest was introduced. When the male finalists paraded down the catwalk at London Grosvenor House Hotel, they were greeted with screams of appreciation and suggestive remarks from excited females in the audience. When the Misses' turn came, they were met by polite applause from the demure, bashful males in the room.

It is an increasingly typical pattern. According to Justine Frishmann, leadsinger with Elastica, her male fans tend to be friendly, shy, enthusiastic types. "I've certainly never felt like I'm being approached sexually." However, her boyfriend, Damon Albarn, leadsinger with Blur, finds that his fans are far more forward. "Girls can be a lot more obsessed about people in bands," says Frishmann. "I don't think it's very respectful for a boy to go up to a girl and just try it on with her, but it's more accepted if a girl does it to a bloke."

As if to prove that point, *Sky magazine* this month sent three female reporters off to a series of pubs and parties to try and pull men with naff male chat-up lines such as, "Cheer up, love, it may never happen". The resulting article was extremely funny, but its most revealing moments were the descriptions of the three writers themselves. "Babe One" was Sylvia, "the heat-seeking missile of the pulling world. Nigh-on insatiable, yet ruthlessly selective." Toni was "utterly powerless to resist the seduction of things she hasn't tried before". And Vicki was "possessed of a healthy sexual appetite. Better still, the concept of shame is meaningless to her."

These outrageously sexist and exploitative phrases were not the work of vile, male journo-pigs. They were produced, with tongues firmly placed in cheeks, by an editorial team, led by the magazine's editor, Angela Holden. They demonstrate that the upsurge of apparently laddish behaviour among young women has not been accompanied by any desire to seem masculine or butch. Quite the contrary, the self-confessed babes and chicks who populate *Sky's* pages are unashamedly "gooey and giggly and girly".

Not so long ago, the very word "girl" was considered to be offensive by the right-on thought police. Those days are long gone, says Holden. "Young women are tired of being the standard-bearers for political correctness in the media. The idea that they are the long-suffering, wimpy victims of men's appalling behaviour is an annoying stereotype. You don't have to have a personality like a wet herbal tea bag."

Holden agrees that young women are acting in ways that were once reserved for men. "Men don't have the monopoly on fun. Once you accept that, all the other behaviour follows." However, she dismisses talk of faux-blokedom. "It's all about expressing your femaleness." Girls will call themselves babes or chicks for exactly the same reason gays call themselves queers: they are reclaiming sexist terms for themselves.

They are reclaiming sexist clothes, too. The Wonderbra phenomenon – based on a marketing campaign that was devised entirely by women – is a true sign of the times. The girls who wear these triumphs of mammary engineering are acting in an assertive, self-determined way that is traditionally masculine, while expressing their assertion in a manner that is undeniably feminine.

This is a difficult concept to grasp for those men still wedded to the notion of female victimisation. An increasing number of the complainants protesting to the Advertising Standards Authority over ads such as those for Wonderbra are men. It is no surprise: the idea that women are helpless pawns of a brutal patriarchy is deeply reassuring to the right-on male. He loves knowing that he could oppress women if he wasn't such a wonderful, caring guy.

Self-confident chicks who refuse to see themselves as anybody's victim are a very different matter. Personally, I think they are great, if only because their hearty commitments to bad behaviour destroys for once and for all the notion that there is something uniquely bestial about the male psyche.

In any case, we should not necessarily take the new ladettes at face value. Sarah Palmer is a market researcher who last year helped compile a survey on Wild Women for [an agency]. She found the young women she interviewed to be ultra-confident on the surface. But, she noted:" There is a lot of bluster beneath the confidence. There is enormous pressure to be sorted out, be cool, have a career, have a relationship. It's very difficult."

Any lad would understand. His cockiness, too, is all based on bluff or bluster. He is all mouth and no trousers. The ladette, meanwhile, is all mouth and no miniskirt. And what could be more equal than that?

Hen behaving badly.

Info

Lad culture and ladette culture – British boys and girls gone wild

'Lad culture' is a subculture commonly associated with music of the 1990s and the sitcom "Men Behaving Badly". It also involves a liking for alcoholic beverages, especially lager, fast automobiles and men's magazines.
The term ladette refers to a female incarnation of the lad stereotype who engages in activities that are traditionally associated with boisterous males, such as rowdy football fandom, or lager drinking.
In an interview entitled "'Ladette Culture' on the Rise", Colin Pritchard, professor at Bournemouth University's Institute of Health and Community Studies, said, "the bad news is that 20 years ago boys drugged, drank, smoked, truanted, stole, vandalized and fought more than girls. [...] Today it is very different. Girls now significantly smoke and binge-drink more than boys. They truant, steal and fight at similar rates to boys but have started under-age sex earlier than boys."
(abcnews, 25 May 2006)

Vocabulary

Title: to call s.o.'s bluff: to tell s.o. to do what they have threatened because you do not believe that they will really do it - **Intro: a bit of a lad**: (spoken) a man that people like even though he behaves rather badly - **to swill** (v.): (informal) to drink s.th. in large amounts - **wolf-whistle** (v.): to whistle like men sometimes do to show that they think a woman is attractive - **to relinquish** (v.): to give up - **blokish** (adj.): if you do blokish things you behave in a traditionally male way - **2 be made of sterner stuff**: to have a strong character and be more determined than other people to succeed in a difficult situation - **5 to be jailed** (v.): to be sent to prison - **17 ale buff** (n.): s.o. who loves that type of beer and knows a lot about it - **26 faux** (adj.): artificial, but made to look real - **28 to leer** (v.): to look at s.o. in an unpleasant way that shows that you think they are sexually attractive - **29 hunk** (n.): (informal) a sexually attractive man with a big strong body - **29 beefy** (adj.): big and strong - **33 appreciation** (n.): pleasure you feel when you realize that s.th. is good, useful, or well done - **36 demure** (adj.): /dimjuə/ quiet, serious and well-behaved; used especially about women in the past - **36 bashful** (adj.): easily embarrassed - **46 to try it on with s.o.**: (BrE spoken) to attempt to start a sexual relationship with s.o. - **50 naff** (adj.): (BrE informal) silly, here because it shows a lack of good taste - **50 chat-up line** (n.): (BrE) s.th. that s.o. says in order to start a conversation with s.o. they think is sexually attractive - **50 to pull** (v.): (BrE spoken) to attract s.o. in order to have sex with them or spend the evening with them - **55 nigh-on** (adv.): (old-fashioned) almost - **55 insatiable** (adj.): always wanting more and more of s.th. - **56 ruthless** (adj.): determined to get what you want - **61 vile** (adj.): extremely unpleasant or bad - **61 journo** (n.): sl for journalist - **65 laddish** (adj.): (BrE) a young man who is laddish likes spending time with other men, drinking alcohol and enjoying things like sport, sex, and music - **66 butch** (adj.): (informal) a woman who is butch looks, behaves, or dresses like a man; a man who is butch seems big and strong, and typically male - **67 babe** (n.): (spoken informal) a word for an attractive young woman - **67 chick** (n.): (informal) a word meaning a young woman, that some people think is offensive - **68 gooey** (adj.): showing your love for s.o. in a way that other people think is silly - **71 right on** (adj.):(BrE informal) s.o. who is right on supports social justice, equal rights, the protection of the environment etc.; often used to show disapproval because s.o. does this in an extreme (politically correct) way - **89 mammary** (adj.): (technical) connected with or relating to the breasts - **98 pawn** (n.): s.o. who is used by a more powerful person or group and has no control of the situation - **107 bestial** (adj.): (literary) behaving like an animal, especially in a cruel way - **113 bluster** (n.): loud and angry speech that is not really impressive - **117 cockiness** (n.): too much confidence about yourself and your abilities, especially in a way that annoys other people

Explanations

Intro: sugar and spice: refers to a nursery rhyme about the differences between girls and boys (see p. 5) - **3 AA**: Automobile Association; a British organisation which provides services for people who own cars - **13 The Brewers' and Licenced Retailers' Association**: this association published a beer and pub guide - **15 Babycham**: BrE, tdmk., a sweet, sparkling, alcoholic drink which comes in a small bottle. It is usually considered to be a woman's drink. - **17f. Carlsberg-Tetley**: tdmk., famous beer brewery - **39 Elastica**: a punk band, famous on both sides of the Atlantic in 1995; they split up in 2001 - **43 Blur**: an equally famous Britpop band in the 1990s; Justine and Damon, who were often called the King and Queen of Britpop, have also split up -

60 sexist (adj.): referring to the attitudes of s.o. who believes that one sex is weaker, less intelligent, or less important than the other; see info on p. 55 - **73 political correctness**: a code of language, behaviour and attitudes that are carefully chosen not to offend or insult anyone - **86 Wonderbra**: tdmk. for a push-up bra - **96 Advertising Standards Authority (ASA)**: a British organisation which controls the activities of the advertising industry. If people think an advertisement is wrong or offensive, they can complain to this organisation, which may decide that the advertisement should not be used again.

Awareness

1 When you go out to a disco or pop concert next time, watch the behaviour of young women and young men and try to explain the differences.

2 When you go through some British (seaside) towns you will frequently find signs which declare an area to be an alcohol-free zone. Can you imagine why this is so? Do similar phenomena exist in your home country?

3 Make a list of adjectives that you think apply to men and another one that you think apply to women. Compare your lists in class.

Comprehension

4 What does the text say about the changing crime rates among women and men?

5 How does male/female behaviour differ when they are spectators at beauty competitions or listeners in the pop business?

6 To what extent has the behaviour of young women changed against the code of behaviour of young women in previous generations?

7 Why is the male author of the article glad about the changes?

8 Characterise the 'ladette'.

Analysis

9 Analyse examples of colloquial speech and slang in the text and what they contribute to the tone in which the article is presented.

10 Determine the text form of this article.

11 Analyse to what extent it becomes obvious that the author of this article is a man.

Project

12 Work with your neighbour and imagine you have seen your dream man/dream woman. Design your chat-up line and then try it out in a roleplay.

Internet Projects

13 Check www.imdb.com and find out about "Britain's most successful sitcom of the 1990s" '(British) Men Behaving Badly' and how it can be related to the sociological concept that is called 'lad culture'.

14 Check www.imdb.com for ITV1's latest reality show "Ladettes to Ladies" in which "10 women compete to transform themselves (in Eliza Doolittle style) from ladettes to ladies".

15 The following advertisement was published in the Internet: "Notorious ladettes wanted for 2nd series at ITV's Finishing School – contact: michelle.woods@rdfmedia.com." Find out about the casting conditions.
Wikipedia quotes several links to investigate into lad culture:
"/wiki/Subculture"\
"/wiki/Britpop"\
"/wiki/Sitcom"\
"/wiki/Men_Behaving_Badly"\

13

"A bad victory for women"

In this feature story novelist and journalist India Knight takes a critical look at ex-banker Laura Zubulake, who successfully sued for sex discrimination. - *The Sunday Times*, 10 April 2005.

Last week, Laura Zubulake, a 44-year-old former Wall Street banker, won £ 15.6m in a sex discrimination case. A jury in New York decided her former employer UBS AG, Europe s largest bank, had mistreated her because of her gender, and got rid of her when she complained.

"The message for all senior women on Wall Street is not to be afraid to stand up and speak out when they feel they are being treated differently," a triumphant Zubulake said afterwards.

Leaving aside the faintly troubling question of why women should be considered "senior", as in "ancient" at the age of 44, I wonder how much cases such as these - London has an ongoing spate of them, too, though the amounts awarded so far have been smaller - really help women.

Obviously abuses of power need curbing and equally obviously sexist bullying in the workplace is reprehensible. But £ 15.6m is a huge amount of money. You'd really have to be called an awful lot of names.

I wouldn't begrudge the amount if it went to the hard-working immigrant who gets daily physical abuse and dog mess shoved through his letter box for years on end. I'd also quite like it if some poor put-upon drudge snuck it off her rich philandering husband.

Needless to say, I'd be delighted to see victims of child abuse and rape, for instance, get even a fraction of this amount as compensation for their suffering. But a woman who earns £ 350,000 a year and gets the hump because some bloke is mean to her at work? Oh, please.

Can you imagine men suing for vast amounts of money because their boss didn't ask them to the pub last Friday night, called them a dickhead or laughed at their tie? Can you imagine what would happen if schoolchildren sued every time someone teased them? If every woman had a fit when someone made an off-colour joke?

There is no doubt that financial centres such as Wall Street, or the City of London, are not what you'd call wildly women-friendly environments in which to work. Equally there is no doubt that any woman who finds herself in such a traditionally male bastion as the City or the law courts - from memory, the newspaper newsrooms used to be pretty terrifying too - will cotton on swiftly to the fact that the sensitive-little-flower schtick isn't going to be much of a winner.

In order not to keel over with shock or horror every two seconds, you quickly need to develop the hide of an especially robust rhinoceros. And you do. Certainly, Zubulake must have done so for the years leading up to her sacking. How else to explain her position at UBS as one of its best-paid executives?

Yet central to Zubulake's case, which has taken three years to resolve, was the mimsy complaint that Matthew Chapin, her immediate boss, had said about her: "She's too old and ugly and she can't do the job." Which, admittedly, isn't very nice.

On the other hand, it wouldn't necessarily have one weeping into one's lace hanky before scurrying sobbing to the loo, either. Nor would an offer to join colleagues and clients at a strip joint (which left Zubulake "appalled").

She also said she was regularly patronised in front of colleagues, denied lucrative accounts, discriminated against by not being asked to a couple of baseball and golf games where clients would be present and - weirdly - discriminated against by not being asked to another strip club.

Oh, and she didn't like the position of her desk, which

was placed - eew! - among the lowly PAs. No matter how I look at this, for every complaint that sounds vaguely justified there are two that just sound pathetic.

The bank's defence, unusually enough, had the ring of truth about it. It was that Zubulake's boss was horrible to everyone, not just her. His male colleagues had also complained about him, but interestingly none had gone so far as to take legal action. This is what is so madly irritating about cases like these. Women claim they want nothing more than to be treated equally and then, the second they are teased and bullied as equals, they run screaming to the courts.

It just looks so wet apart from anything else. Either don't bother with the pretence of equality - there's nothing wrong with saying "I want to be treated very nicely at all times, please, because I'm a girl" - or continue clamouring for equality but deal with it like a grown-up when it comes, warts and all.

In this case dealing with it "like a grown-up" means dealing with it like a man, because women don't seem to be very good at confronting the realities of equality. When push comes to shove, they seem to be, for want of a better expression, all mouth and no trousers.

This not to say there is no such thing as sexual discrimination in the City, because clearly there is an awful lot of it. Apart from anything else, men who work there are often mad, sad and greedy. They wouldn't be one's companions of choice, let's say.

Everyone knows this. But it is also true that stupid men are everywhere, and making inappropriate jokes about someone's chest or speculating about their sex life happens quite often in office environments.

In the City, such admittedly tiresome banter cost Merrill Lynch £ 1m last year after Elizabeth Weston complained. In the real world it happens every two seconds. And no, of course you don't have to like it, but you don't have to be total feeble sap about it either.

Some might say that Zubulake has had the last laugh, and I suppose financially she may have. She can be as jubilant as she likes about her heaps of cash (though UBS is planning to appeal), but she should pipe down about the great service she has done sisterhood.

For all her triumphant rhetoric, cases such as this one set women back decades. Put very basically, Zubulake won £ 15.6m because she didn't much care for being called plain.

Try as I might, I can't for the life of me see in what possible way this constitutes any kind of victory.

"No, equal pay doesn't mean you'll be getting the same as me."

Vocabulary

6 senior (adj.): having a higher position, level or rank - **11 ancient** (adj.): having existed for a long time - **13 spate** (n.): a large number of similar things that happen in a short period of time, especially bad things - **16 to curb** (v.): to control or limit s.th. in order to prevent it from having a harmful effect - **18 reprehensible** (adj.): s.th. that deserves criticism - **19 to call s.o. names**: to use insulting names for s.o. - **20 to begrudge** (v.): to feel angry or upset with s.o. because they have s.th. which you think they do not deserve - **22 dog mess** (n.): solid waste from a dog - **23 put-upon** (adj.): s.o. who feels that other people are treating them unfairly by expecting them to do too much - **23 drudge** (n.): s.o. who does hard boring work - **24 philandering** (adj.): (old-fashioned) having sex with many women without intending to have any serious relationships - **28 to get the hump**: to feel angry or upset - **30 to sue** (v.): to make a legal claim against s.o., especially for money - **32 dickhead** (n.): an offensive word for a stupid, annoying person, especially a man - **41 law court** (n.): a room or building where legal cases are judged - **42f. to cotton on** (v.): (informal) to begin to understand s.th. - **44 schtick** (n.): a typical quality or feature that s.o. is famous for - **52 mimsy** (adj.): prim or affected, over-refined - **57 lace hanky** (n.): a handkerchief trimmed with fine cloth made with patterns of many very small holes - **57 to scurry** (v.): to move quickly with small steps - **59 strip joint** (n.): (informal) a strip club - **61 to patronise** (v.): to talk to s.o. in a way which seems friendly but shows that you think they are not as intelligent or do not know as much as you - **68 lowly** (adj.): low in rank, importance or social class - **70 pathetic** (adj.): s.th. or s.o. that is so useless, unsuccessful, or weak that they annoy you - **80 wet** (adj.): (BrE) s.o. who does not have a strong character - **84 to clamour for s.th.** (v.): to demand s.th. loudly - **85 warts and all**: (informal) including all the faults or unpleasant things - **89 when push comes to shove**: (BrE, spoken) if a situation becomes very difficult or action needs to be taken - **94 greedy** (adj.): always wanting more food, money, power, possessions etc.than you need - **104 sap** (n.): (informal) a stupid person who is easy to deceive or treat badly - **108 to pipe down** (v.): to stop talking or making a noise, and become calmer and less excited - **109 sisterhood** (n.): a special loyal relationship among women who share the same ideas and aims, especially among feminists

Explanations

1f. Wall Street: a street in New York City which is the influential American center for money matters and the buying and selling of business shares - **3 UBS**: a global investment banking and securities firm - **37 City** (of London): an area in Central London which is the British centre for money matters - **68 PA**: (BrE) personal assistant, secretary - **100f. Merrill Lynch**: one of the world's leading financial management and advisory companies

India Knight, the daughter of a Pakistani mother and a Belgian father, was born in Brussels in 1965. She is a novelist and a journalist and writes a weekly column for the Sunday Times, in which she comments on issues of general interest, among other topics on gender-related questions. She has also written a collection of essays and two novels which deal with the role of women. In an interview she stated that "being neatly married and living in your little suburbian house is not necessarily a valid solution" to life's problems. She lives in London with her two children.

Background Reading 1

Sexual harassment

The Equal Opportunities Commission (EOC) defines sexual harassment in the following way:

Sexual harassment is behaviour which has always existed but which, in the past, has been little talked about, much less given the serious attention it deserves. Indeed, it is often treated as something to be tolerated and passed off as being part of normal working relations between men and women, as if it were harmless fun. However, to the victims – more commonly women, but sometimes men – sexual harassment is no laughing matter.

Sexual harassment can take many forms, all of which are unacceptable to its victims. It may include unreciprocated and unwelcome comments, looks, physical contact or suggestions such as requests for sexual favours. It is behaviour which is objectionable or offensive to the victims and which might threaten their job security or create an intimidating or hostile working environment which may very well hinder the victim in his or her work performance. Sexual harassment may be symptomatic of the working environment, which tolerates certain attitudes towards women, such as the dis-play of pictures of naked women.

Sexual harassment may also amount to indecent assault (i.e. a hostile act accompanied by circumstances of indecency) which is a criminal offence and in such circumstances individuals should seek legal advice as soon as possible.

EOC. *Sex Discrimination Decisions.* Leaflet No. 16

Sexual harassment has been recognized as a problem by feminists since the 1970s. It includes a large area of behaviour ranging from verbal to physical abuse and rape. It is a salacious topic which often gets a lot of press coverage, but which was not recognized as an appropriate matter of concern in Britain until the early 1980s. It is a vexed issue for workplace managers and negotiators. Behaviour that most women would define as harassment is often considered harmless fun by many men.

Women against Sexual Harassment (WASH) was formed in 1984 and is the main feminist group campaigning on the issue. WASH defines sexual harassment as behaviour of a sexual nature which is unwelcome and unreciprocated and which might threaten job security and create a stressful and intimidating environment. This behaviour may include comments, looks, jokes, suggestions, pin-ups, and physical contact ranging from touching to pinching and rape. In the meantime trade unions have taken up this issue as well.

For further information, read: Joni Lovenduski/Vicky Randall, *Contemporary Feminist Politics. Women and Power in Britain* (Oxford: Oxford University Press, 1993).

Background Reading 2

Equality at work

The Sex Discrimination Act (SDA) was passed in 1975 to prevent sex discrimination, i.e. the unfair treatment of a person because they are of a particular sex, esp. in matters of employment and education. The Sex Discrimination Act gives rights to both men and women.
The Act says:

It is unlawful to discriminate on the grounds of sex or marriage directly or indirectly in arrangements made for determining who should be offered employment, on the terms on which employment is offered, or by refusing or deliberately omitting to offer employment. (Section 6(1)(a)(b)(c).)

The Equal Opportunities Commission (EOC) was set up by Parliament in 1975 to eliminate sex discrimination in employment, education and training opportunities, in the provision of goods, facilities, services and accomodation - and generally to encourage equal opportunities for men and women in many other areas of activity.

Finding a Job:

There should be nothing in the wording or presentation of advertisements for jobs covered by the Act to give the impression that only men, or women, or single people are required. If you are interested in a job appearing in an advertisement that seems to be discriminatory, there are two things you can do:

- tell the EOC about the advertisement who can advise you whether it is unlawful and can take certain action themselves;
- and, if appropriate, apply for the job anyway (in writing if you can).

In the Job:

You are entitled to equal access on equal terms to promotion, transfer, training and to any other benefits, facilities or services provided by your employer. This covers the arrangements made for selecting who should be promoted, transferred or trained, as well as the actual selection itself.

You are entitled to an equal chance to join a trade union or professional organisation, to equal terms of membership and to equal access to any benefits, facilities or services it provides. Your membership cannot be ended, or its conditions altered, nor can you be treated unfavourably in any other way on grounds of your sex or marriage.

What to Do:

- Don't just decide to leave your job.
- Use your employer's grievance procedure.
- See your trade union representative if you have one.
- Write to or ring the EOC.
  - They can give you free advice and in many cases financial assistance for legal representation before an Industrial Tribunal.
  - All enquiries are dealt with in the strictest confidence and no contact is ever made either with your employer or the press without your express permission.

The Time Limit:

It is vital to remember that to enforce the law by taking your case to an Industrial Tribunal, you must lodge your complaint with the Central Office of Industrial Tribunals (COIT) before the end of the period of 3 months beginning when the act complained of was done. If you think you may have been unlawfully discriminated against, therefore, there is little time to lose.

The Industrial Tribunal:

This is a relatively informal "court" which will usually take place somewhere near to where you live. There is a legally qualified chairman [!] and two ordinary members of the public, who have knowledge or experience of industry or commerce. There is a free booklet, "How to Present your Own Case at an Industrial Tribunal" which can be obtained from the EOC and which will help you understand the procedures involved.

Deborah Lambert (in association with the EOC), *Equality at Work. A Guide to the Employment Provisions of the Sex Discriminations Act* 1975, pp. 1-11.

Info

Sexism

A word coined, on the analogy of racism, for a deep-rooted, often unconscious system of beliefs, attitudes, and institutions in which distinctions between people's intrinsic worth are made on the grounds of their sex and sexual roles. Whether consciously or not, the sexist sees woman (or man) as inferior, and behaves accordingly. As with racism, the term – though not the phenomenon – tends in practice to be restricted to one-way attitudes only, i.e. to male sexism. In the aggressive form of sexism known as 'male chauvinism' the paradigm is one of an assumed innate male supremacy in all the most important areas of social activity (with the possible exception of child-rearing), accompanied by a predisposition to treat women as anonymous objects for male sexual pleasure.

The Fontana Dictionary of Modern Thought (London: Fontana, 1988), pp. 774f.

"And we'd have someone to grope!!"

Awareness

1 Translate the illustration on p. 54 and the cartoon above into two prose stories.
2 The borderline between flattery and offence is a rather thin one. If construction workers at a building site wolf-whistle at a woman is that flattery or offence?
3 List up examples of sexual discrimination.

Comprehension

4 Why did Ms Zubulake sue her former employer?
5 How much compensation money did she get?
6 What does the author reproach Ms Zubulake with?
7 What comparison does the author draw between Wall Street and the City (of London)?
8 List up what, according to the author, are still male bastions.
9 How do the men who work in those bastions behave?
10 What is meant by behaving "like a grown-up" (l. 84)?

Analysis

11 Write a character sketch of Ms Zubulake from the author's point of view.
12 Analyse linguistic and stylistic devices in this article which reveal the author's opinion of Ms Zubulake.
13 Characterise the general tone in the article and explain how it is achieved.

Opinion

14 Do you agree with Ms Zubulake's opinion that "not being asked to [a] strip club" (ll. 65f.) is a sign of discrimination?
15 Whose side are you on? Give detailed reasons for your opinion.
16 Write a letter to India Knight in which you comment on her article and the implications it evokes: India.Knight@sunday-times.co.uk

Internet Project

17 Go to www.eoc.org.uk and find out about the more than 30-year-old history of the Equal Opportunities Commission and the procedures of how to take a claim to the employment tribunal or local court. The info background reading on pp. 54f. might also be useful.

14

Adriaane Pielou

"Prattle of the sexes"

It is a well-known platitude that men and women cannot understand each other. Scientists have now found out the reason why: they do not speak the same language. Adriaane Pielou has interviewed Deborah Tannen, whose book *You Just Don't Understand: Women and Men in Conversation* (Virago, 1991), interprets the linguistic behaviour of the sexes. – *You Magazine* 1991, pp. 64-66.

The scene's familiar. She says: 'You don't listen.' He says: 'You never get to the point.' And that, says Deborah Tannen, is the fundamental difference between the sexes. For when it comes to conversation, they don't speak the same language.

Men: they cringe at the prospect of discussing anything personal, grumble they're being nagged when asked to take out the rubbish and, if they lose their way, rage at the suggestion they ask for the way.

Women: they read things into the most innocuous comment, get upset when their man says 'I' rather than 'we' and demand impossibly detailed reports of every conversation they miss – who said what and how they looked when they said it.

And, says American sociologist Deborah Tannen, it will all go on like this, each sex bristling at the other's peculiar ways, until we wake up to the simple truth – men and women don't speak the same language.

It's not so much that the vocabulary and grammar we use are different, she explains in her New York apartment. The differences lie in the way men and women talk.

Since our lives are lived as a series of conversations, it's her belief that we start to appreciate and understand these differences – and the reasons behind them – the better. [...]

Tall, gentle, immediately likable and mercifully spouting little of the jargon you'd expect of one of the world's leading lights in her field, Deborah Tannen is Professor of Linguistics at the University of Georgetown, Washington DC. For more than 20 years, she has studied how people talk – what they mean by what they say and how it can be construed and often misunderstood.

Eavesdropping in restaurants, collecting friends' anecdotes, watching hundreds of hours of taped conversation ... all in the name of research.

The thrust of this study is that women use language to enhance intimacy, men to assert independence. Women, concerned primarily with making connections with people, regard conversation as a way to share feelings, create bonds and explore possible solutions to common problems.

Men are concerned primarily with status, and prefer discussion of facts to dissection of feelings. Since feelings suggest vulnerability and thus inferiority, men see conversation as another way of scoring points. The lost-in-the-car scenario is an illustration of this. You know the scene – it's universal. Invited to a party, a couple have been driving round in circles for the address which he is sure is nearby. She is fuming because he insists on trying to find the address himself instead of stopping to ask directions. Check the dialogue:

She: I'm sure we came down this street ten minutes ago.

He: No, this is right. I know where I'm going.

She: Shouldn't we just stop and ask someone?

He: There is no point in asking anyone. They won't know the place. They'll just send us off in the wrong direction.

She: Well, even if they did, we could always ask someone else.

He: Look, if you don't like the way I'm driving, why don't you walk to your fat friend's party?

So, who's right? Neither, says Deborah Tannen. This sort of exchange simply typifies the different approaches men and women have to asking for information. Since women are so used to asking for help, refusing to ask directions makes no sense to the wife. To her, asking for and receiving directions reinforces the bond between people. But in her husband's hierarchical world, where every man has his antennae rolled out to who's up or down, driving round until he finds the way himself is the reasonable thing to do. Men are comfortable with giving help or information, but not with receiving it. So asking for directions would make the husband feel he was dropping in status by revealing his lack of knowledge.

Long-winded? In the world of socio-linguism, this is only scratching the surface of the male-female conversational anomalies lying behind that brief exchange. Mention any aspect of everyday chat and Deborah can cite the ways men's and women's attitudes to it differ.

Take politeness. Men consider it subservient, women sensitive. Boasting. Men boast as a matter of course, battling to gain or maintain that all-important status. Women, who tend to gain acceptance with each other by appearing the same as, not better than, everyone else, take care never to boast.

Apparently, the main difference in the way we communicate is in the crucial matter of the 'meta-message,' the unspoken attitudes, thoughts and intentions behind the main 'message' – what is actually said. And while fact-oriented men tend to listen to the message, feeling-orientated women tend to listen for the subtler message.

For instance:

She: Why don't you ask me how my day was?

He: If you've got something to tell me, tell me. Why do you have to be invited?

She's fed up because she wants to hear the meta-message of interest – evidence that he cares how her day went, regardless of what actually happened. And he, concerned principally with the fact-exchanging aspect of conversation, can't understand what she's complaining about.

Which – added to another Tannen discovery that once at home men feel relieved of the otherwise constant pressure to compete conversationally – helps explain why women complain their husbands never talk to them. Or never listen.

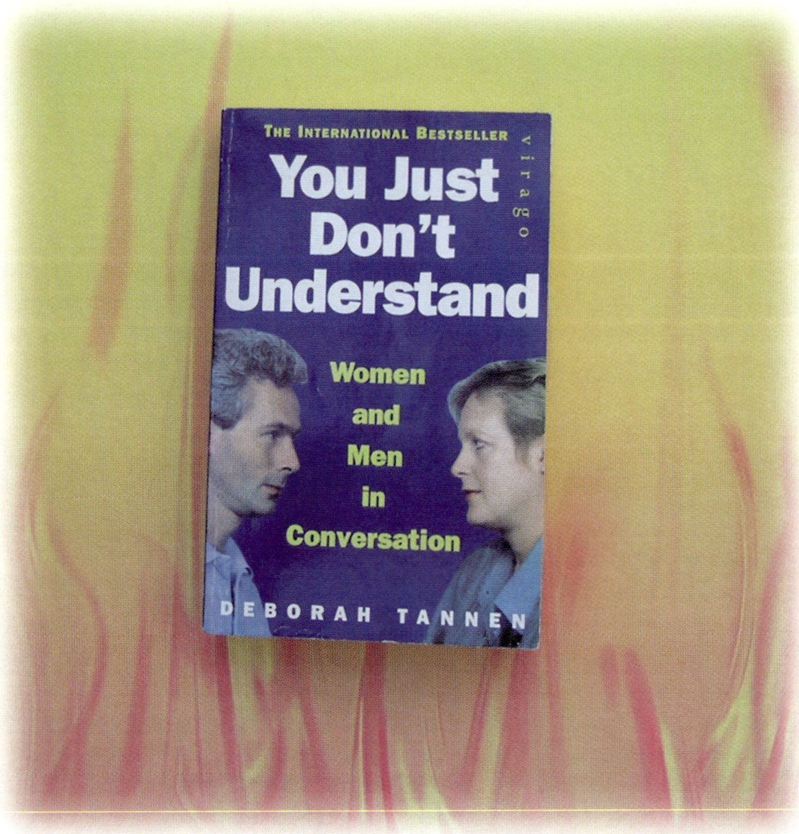

Vocabulary

Title: prattle (n.): derogatory for childish, unimportant or meaningless talk - **6 to cringe** (v.): informal for to have a very uncomfortable feeling of shame or dislike - **7 to nag** (v.): to annoy or try to persuade (s.o.) by continuously finding fault and complaining - **8 to rage** (v.): to be in a wild uncontrollable anger - **10 innocuous** (adj.): not likely to or intended to harm or offend - **16 to bristle** (v.): to make one's hair stand up stiffly - **23 to appreciate** (v.): to understand fully, to recognize - **26 mercifully** (adv.): happening by good luck and changing a situation - **27 to spout** (v.): informal or derogatory for to pour out in a stream of words - **27 jargon** (n.): often derogatory for difficult or strange language which uses words known only to the members of a certain group - **28 leading light** (n.): informal for a person of importance or influence - **32 to construe** (v.): formal for to place a particular meaning on s.th. - **33 eavesdropping** (n.): listening secretly, esp. to other people's conversation - **36 thrust** (n.): the main meaning or central point - **37 to enhance** (v.): to increase in strength or amount - **37 to assert** (v.): to make a claim to; defend (a right or claim) by forceful action - **40 bond** (n.): s.th. that unites two or more people or groups, such as a shared feeling or interest - **43 dissection** (n.): a very careful study, esp. so as to find the faults - **44 vulnerability** (n.): the state of being easily harmed, hurt or wounded - **44 inferiority** (n.): the state of being not good or less good in quality or value - **45 to score** (v.): to gain - **46 scenario** (n.): a description of a possible course of action or events - **49 to fume** (v.): to be angry or restless, but often without expres-sing one's feelings fully - **67 to reinforce** (v.): to add strength or support to; make stronger or firmer - **69 antenna** (n.): here one's feelers; plural: antennae - **75 long-winded** (adj.): /lɒŋ'wɪndɪd/ going on too long and using too many words - **77 anomaly** (n.): a person, thing, or situation that is different from the usual or accepted type - **81 subservient** (adj.): derogatory for habitually willing to do what others want; tending to obey others' wishes - **82 sensitive** (adj.): knowing or being conscious of the feelings of others - **82 boasting** (n.): an act of talking with unreasonable or unpleasant pride - **88 crucial** (adj.): of decisive importance - **100 regardless of** (adv.): without worrying about or taking account of

Explanations

88f. meta-message: When people do or say s.th. they send out a message, which is the obvious meaning of the act. At the same time what they do or say sends meta-messages, i.e. information about the relations among the people involved, and their attitudes about what they are saying and doing and the people they are saying or doing it to.

Adriaane Pielou interviewed Deborah Tannen, Professor of Linguistics at Georgetown University in Washington, D.C. The interview was motivated by the publication of Tannen's book *You Just Don't Understand: Men and Women in Conversation* (London: Virago, 1991). Tannen received her Ph.D. in linguistics from the University of California, Berkeley and has been awarded fellowships and grants from many organisations, including The Rockefeller Foundation and the National Science Foundation. With eleven books and over seventy articles to her credit, she has been invited to lecture all over the world. She is Associate Editor of the journal *Text* and is on the editorial boards of all the major journals in her field.

Awareness

1 Compare the title of this text with that of text 4 and speculate on the connections.
2 Have you ever noticed any differences in the ways men and women talk? Compare your observations and experiences.

Comprehension

3 What - according to Tannen - is the basic difference between the sexes?
4 In what ways do men and women differ when they speak?
5 How is the linguist D. Tannen described by the author?
6 From which sources did Tannen get her information?
7 What is the scene of the couple that has lost their way meant to signify?
8 Whose side does Tannen take?
9 Give an example of the idea of "meta-message" as used in the text.
10 How – according to Tannen – do men feel when they are at home?

Analysis

11 Juxtapose the differences between male and female ways of talking enlarged upon in this text.
12 Explain the difference between message and meta-message by referring to examples from the text.
13 What elements in the text can be seen as evidence that this is a summarized interview?

Opinion

14 The conclusion to be drawn from this article is that men and women cannot communicate. Do you share this opinion? Do you find this depressing or do you see any cause for optimism? Give reasons for your opinion.
15 Compare your results under question 2 with Tannen's statements. Do you agree with her? Give reasons for your agreement or disagreement.

Project

16 If you were a marriage counsellor what advice would you give to the couple whose two dialogues are reported in the article to help them communicate?

Further Reading

17 Read Deborah Tannen's *Gender & Discourse* (New York and Oxford, 1994)

15

David Cohen

"A Gender for Change"

In his book *Being a Man* David Cohen, a film maker and journalist, investigates what changes the women's movement has brought to the lives of men and tries to answer the question of whether there have been any serious male responses to the feminist challenge. - David Cohen, *Being a Man* (London: Routledge, 1990), pp. 191f.

Harmony at last – friends at last?

It is all too clear that the glorious, if nebulous, revolution [of 1968] never came. When students were marching, the one item that was not on the agenda was sex roles. Oddly, it could be argued that one of the most important social changes of the last twenty years has been precisely in those areas that were ignored in the demos and street battles of 1968. Despite many setbacks and disappointments, feminists have succeeded in making clear the justice and necessity of equal rights and opportunities for women. Slowly, the attitudes of men are changing. I am not suggesting some Panglossian scenario, but what is clear is that there have been large changes in the way women think of themselves and in the way we all view relationships between the sexes. [...] Macho itself has become something of a joke. Only those who are insecure have to put on the macho. Masculine heroes are no longer so old-style masculine, and, as I tried to suggest, one of the problems men face is that there is confusion of role models to identify with. Even as apparently diehard a hero as Clint Eastwood, heir to John Wayne, has in some of his films tried to cope with feminist heroines.

I've tried to analyse psychological evidence which shows that many men are willing to change and that it is no longer accurate to claim that hard men are exclusively interested in things while sensitive women are interested in people. Rather, what we know (which is limited and flawed) shows that, for both sexes, relationships are central. We judge the success and failure of much of our lives by the success and failure of relationships. I don't deny the evidence of the violence of men. Nevertheless, the now orthodox feminist argument that men don't care about women seems wrong. Some men don't know how to care, but to feather and tar the whole sex seems extreme. [...]

Given no official initiative, there are limits to what individual couples can achieve. Feminism started out with a political agenda. It involved equal opportunities, equal rights, and equal pay. These have all become left-wing issues in the last twenty years, but, ironically, in Britain, the main left-wing organization, the Labour movement, has done little to promote them. Women trade unionists have often complained of how hard they have had to fight to achieve any measure of equality within the union movement. There were women cabinet ministers, and, indeed, a woman prime minister long before there was a woman general secretary of a union. Brenda Dean, the first woman general secretary is the head of a small union. It is surprising that feminists have succeeded to the extent they have given the fact that the Right opposes most their demands – women shouldn't be seen as an oppressed class – while the Left concedes the justice of their case but takes little action – working class men are perceived by their leaders as having too much to lose. (We won't be mean and ask just how much working class leaders have to lose.)

One of the failures of feminism has been its failure to engage sympathetic men as allies. By focusing almost exclusively on the rights that women need to gain, feminists have seemed to suggest either that men will gain nothing from this at all or that they will lose. The Marxist perspective of many feminist writers has reinforced this trend. If the oppressed are to win freedom, the oppressors must lose power. These tactics are understandable and, given what feminists had to struggle against, perhaps inevitable. The silence and defensiveness of men contributed to this view. Feminism could only succeed against men by making men give up things they wanted. Ergo, men were the enemy even if, in order not to seem too hostile, the official enemy was patriarchy.

Feminism has important achievements but such divisive 'battle of the sexes' tactics are, perhaps, no longer the most effective ones. I have tried to show that men too have a lot to gain by the kind of political and economic changes discussed – but, often, we don't realize it. Feminists ought to attempt to make men see the potential advantages. There will, of course, be large numbers of angry, sneering, or frightened men who will insist that they want the world kept the way it always was. There are, however, many other kinds of men too who, I suspect, have realized that expressing feelings doesn't wreck one's masculinity and that it is wonderful to help look after one's children. Feminists could help by reaching out to them.

Such reaching out is important because some of the changes that are necessary are political changes – and most focus around the way we work.

Vocabulary

1 nebulous (adj.): lacking clear form or expression; vague - **3 item** (n.): a single thing on a list or among a set - **3 agenda** (n.): a list of the subjects to be dealt with or talked about in a meeting - **5 precisely** (adv.): exactly - **7 setback** (n.): s.th. that delays or prevents successful progress - **9 justice** (n.): fairness - **11 Panglossian** (adj.): taking an over-cheerful and optimistic view of the world - **11 scenario** (n.): a description of a possible course of action or events - **14 macho** (adj.): usually derogatory for being or wishing to appear very typical of a man, esp. in being strong, brave, and without gentle feelings - **19 diehard** (n.): a person who opposes change and refuses to accept new ideas even when they are good - **20 heir** (n.): the person who has the legal right to receive the property or title of another person, when that person dies - **27 to flaw** (v.): to make s.th. imperfect, faulty or weak - **36 orthodox** (adj.): generally or officially accepted - **40 to feather and tar** (v.): to put tar on s.o. and then cover them with feathers as a punishment - **42 given** (prep.): if one takes into account - **47 left-wing** (adj.): of a group that favour greater political changes - **48 issue** (n.): a subject to be talked about, argued about or decided - **50 to promote** (v.): to introduce and support - **50 trade unionist** (n.): a member of an organization of workers, esp. in a particular trade or profession, formed to represent their interests and deal as a group with employers - **55 general secretary** (n.): the chief official in charge of runnning an organization - **60 to oppress** (v.): to rule in a hard and cruel way - **60 to concede** (v.): to admit as true, correct or proper, often unwillingly - **62 to perceive** (v.): to have knowledge of s.th. through one of the senses (esp. the sight) or through the mind - **66 sympathetic** (n.): showing agreement or approval - **66 ally** (n.): a person who regularly provides help or support - **70 to reinforce** (v.): to add strength or support to - **74 inevitable** (adj.): which cannot be avoided or prevented from happening - **77 ergo** (adv.): Latin, therefore - **78 hostile** (adj.): showing extreme dislike or disapproval; unfriendly - **78 patriarchy** (n.): a social system in which men hold all the power and use it only for their own advantage - **80 divisive** (adj.): tending to make people argue amongst themselves - **86 sneering** (adj.): speaking or behaving as if s.th. is not worthy of serious attention - **89 to suspect** (v.): to believe to be true or likely - **90 to wreck** (v.): to destroy

Explanations

1 glorious revolution: reminiscent of the Glorious Revolution, the time in British history (1688-89) when King James II was removed from power, and his daughter Mary and her husband William of Orange became joint rulers. It was also called the Bloodless Revolution. - **80 battle of the sexes** (n.): term that has traditionally been applied to the not always amical, sometimes openly hostile relations between the sexes; see also texts 4 and 14

David Cohen combines the personal with the psychological and provides a thoughtful, sometimes amusing discussion of the changing position of men in society. For him, the separation from his wife and the agreement to share looking after their teenage children seems to work fine, especially since Cohen and his ex-wife live only half a mile apart. On the other hand, being a free-lance journalist and film maker he is much more flexible than most fathers, even though he claims that this is only due to the fact that he has made a name for himself in his profession.

Awareness

1 Imagine you were living in an ideal society. What would the perfect relationship between the sexes be like in this utopia?

Comprehension

2 What does Cohen mean by "the glorious [...] revolution" (l. 1)?
3 Explain what the term 'macho' (l. 14) means.
4 How does the author evaluate the current role of men?
5 Express in your own words what Cohen sees as the achievements and the failures of feminism.
6 What differences does he see among male trade unionists?
7 Who is the feminists' main enemy?
8 a) What tactical changes does the author advise feminists to undertake?
b) Why does he suggest these changes?

Analysis

9 Analyse how Cohen portrays the different groups of men he mentions.
10 How does Cohen evaluate the achievements of feminists?
11 Go through the text again and make a list of the possible losses and gains for men and women.

Opinion

12 Cohen mentions various political groups and tendencies. What do you think his political affiliation is? Give reasons for your opinion.
13 Discuss in how far job sharing and child care sharing go together.
14 Do you think that men and women are equal but different? Give reasons for your opinion.

Project

15 Cohen is an avid advocator of job sharing. Carry out a role play between a trade unionist in favour and one against job sharing and discuss the advantages and disadvantages of it.

Abbreviations

n.	=	noun	poet.	=	poetical(ly)
v.	=	verb	s.b.	=	somebody
adj.	=	adjective	s.o.	=	someone
adv.	=	adverb	s.th.	=	something
part.	=	participle	o.s.	=	oneself
prep.	=	preposition	i.e.	=	that is
conj.	=	conjunction	l.	=	line
interj.	=	interjection	ll.	=	lines
sing.	=	singular	p.	=	page
pl.	=	plural	pp.	=	pages
BrE	=	British English	f.	=	and the following (page, line etc.)
AmE	=	American English	ff.	=	and the following (pages, lines etc.)
intro	=	introduction	e.g.	=	for example
mod.	=	modern	tdmk.	=	trademark
esp.	=	especially			

The phonetic transcriptions follow the *Longman Dictionary of Contemporary English (DCE)* and J. C. Wells, *Longman Pronunciation Dictionary.*

Acknowledgements

The material reproduced in this book has been taken from the following sources:

Photographs

Beate Andler, München: p. 63 (middle) - Associated Press GmbH, Frankfurt a. M.: p. 38 - www.johnbirdsall.co.uk: pp. 4 (middle, right), 63 (middle left and right, bottom right) - Hugo Boss AG: p. 43 - Gunhild Brössler, München: p. 4 (left) - www.britainonview.com: p. 23 (top) - Cartoon Stock Ltd., Bath: pp. 40, 44, 45, 48, 51, 52 - CINETEXT, Frankfurt: pp. 21, 22 - Joolz Denby: p. 34 - Mary Evans Picture Library, London: pp. 5 (middle right), 13, 63 (top left and right) - Linda Farwell: p. 59 - Format Partners, London: pp. 5 (middle, bottom right), 54, 63 (middle top, bottom left and middle) - Tim Gravestock, Watford: p. 4 (top) - Sally and Richard Greenhill, London: p. 29 (background) - Christina Hackenberg, München: p. 36 - Robbie Honey: p. 53 - The Hulton Deutsch Collection, London: p. 16 - Interfoto Pressebild-Agentur Bildarchiv, München: p. 6 - iStock International Inc., Calgary: pp. 10, 60 - Library of Congress, Washington D.C.: p. 14 - The New Yorker Magazine, Inc.: p. 33 - Barbara Slowik, München: pp. 4/5 (background), 42/43 (background), 44, 58, 63 (background) - Sophia Smith Collection, Northampton: p. 12 - Zefa Zentrale Farbbild Agentur GmbH, Düsseldorf: p. 30

Texts

The following texts in this collection still under copyright have been reprinted within the terms of § 46 URG via the clearing agency VG Wort. The sources are as follows:
Hodder & Stoughton, London: p. 9 - Secker and Warburg Ltd., London: p. 36 - The Sun, London: p. 42 - The Sunday Times, News International Syndication, London: pp. 38, 47, 51, 53

Except:
Joolz Denby: p. 33 - William Morrow & Company, New York: p. 29 - Alice S. Rossi, University of Massachusetts, Amherst MA: p. 11 - Routledge, London/New York: p. 60 - Solo Syndication Ltd., London: p. 57

We should be very grateful for any information which might assist us in tracing the copyright owners of sources we have been unable to acknowledge.